I0611727

Rigged

"Un-learning Mainstream Financial
Propaganda and Building Your Personal Fortune"

James L Beattey

Rigged

"Un-learning Mainstream Financial Propaganda and Building Your Personal Fortune"

Table of Contents

Acknowledgements

I've never written much more than the occasional term paper in school - so this undertaking was new to me. But over the years, God has put so many wonderful people in my path - people from whom I have learned so much of what has gone into this volume. I have to acknowledge and thank them publicly.

It starts with my parents. Despite my considerable flaws, my mom has loved me unconditionally from day one. She continues to do so today and has taught me much about how to be a parent, a friend, a brother, and a son.

In addition to being a great dad and my personal hero, my dad was also an insurance executive for much of his working life, and I can't help but believe that his vocation left a smoldering ember somewhere deep inside me that has brought me to this point. I have so many memories of my dad in his working years. There was a certain romance to how he conducted himself back then, and I took good mental notes that have helped shape this effort.

My partners, Mark and Dave have helped me sort out my thoughts and have challenged me to build a business that shares my knowledge with other financial professionals around the country.

Finally, to my own family. My beautiful wife, and my two beautiful girls. People thank their families for their "support" all the time. But until you've tackled an endeavor like this, it's hard to know what that support really means.

I can tell you. It means letting me go off in a corner and write when I could be spending time with them. It means convincing me to keep thinking when I'm stuck on a point I can't seem to properly develop. It means encouraging me to carry on - when it would be so much easier to throw in the towel. And it means loving me through the writer's block - and the writer's binges.

Most of all - my family gives me purpose - and for that, I can never thank them enough.

Foreword

There are 32 teams in the National Football League, which means that on each Sunday through the fall, there are 32 individual game plans. Each team and its coaching staff will have considered its personnel, talent, injuries, playing conditions, the opposing team, whether they're at home or away; and will have come up with a formula it believes will lead to a win.

Some will ride the arm of a great passing quarterback; others, their running game; or their defense, even special teams. There may even be a razzle-dazzle play, or a game plan that is totally opposite of what the opponent expected.

Whatever the game plan, sixteen teams will turn out to have been right. And among them, no two game plans will have been the same. What's more, in all likelihood each of those game plans will have been altered during the game in recognition of circumstances that will have changed or that were not anticipated.

When it comes to saving and investing, there are also many game plans that can win. You likely know people who have successfully invested in stocks, bonds, and mutual funds. You know those who have been successful in real estate. Others have made fortunes on commodities, or futures, or options, and countless others. You may be among those who have had some level of success using one or more of these investing strategies or instruments.

We're Americans. We like choice. We like the fact that there are many ways to win the financial game. Each requires skill and knowledge - and because our interests and imaginations respond to different stimuli, the idea that there is more than one path to financial success intrigues us and permits us to blaze our own unique path to the same finish line of financial prosperity.

But losing teams in the NFL can get it wrong this week - and still have next week - or next season to make changes and get it right. You and I - as investors - don't have that same luxury. We have one "fortune-building" season per lifetime. When it's over, there is no more next week or next season - we move right into a phase of life where we live *on* our successes - or we live *with* our failures - whichever the case may be.

In generations past, the requirement to succeed in the accumulation phase was important, but not as important as it is for us today - and there's one simple reason. We'll spend nearly 20 years on average - in retirement. While the accumulation phase of our lives has remained relatively constant through the generations - roughly age 25 to 65 - the retirement phase has expanded substantially.

Did you know for example, that when the Social Security Act was implemented in 1935, the life expectancy of Americans was less than their age of eligibility - 65? What a deal for the government! Collect social security taxes over a person's entire working lifetime, and pay few benefits because a great many of tomorrow's recipients will be dead before they're eligible for benefits. And for those who made it to 65, their life expectancy was much shorter than it is for today's 65-year olds.

The point is this - creating a reliable retirement income stream that can last 20 years or more - when we have the same amount of time in which to create it - becomes a critical task for us. Get it wrong, and the consequences are devastating. Get it right, and the benefits are rewarding.

That may sound obvious, yet millions of Americans will resign themselves to a lifestyle in retirement that is substantially less than they dreamed of. For a few, it will be because they didn't earn enough to adequately fund a comfortable retirement. For others, it will be because their spending desires trumped their need to build an adequate nest egg. But for many - too many - who will have earned adequately and saved consistently - they will fail because they invested poorly.

Now when I say fail - that's a relative term. Few will fail in the sense that they're relegated to eating cat food and skipping meds to pay the gas bill. But many will not achieve the retirement lifestyle, or be the blessing to their kids and grandkids that they would have hoped to have been. They may make it, but their "win" will be the kind that feels more like survival than accomplishment.

And they will not have "failed" on purpose. They will not have failed because they didn't seek professional counsel from good advisors, accountants and planners. They will not have failed because they were uneducated or uninformed. On the contrary.

- They will have hired the best financial advisors - the ones with the nice suits, professional offices, and big stalwart names with deep research benches. Names like Merrill Lynch, Morgan Stanley, Edward Jones, and others.

- They will have read the best publications and kept up on the latest thinking of the Wall Street Journal, Forbes, and Fortune.

- They will have followed the advice of media gurus and pundits like Dave Ramsey, Suze Orman, and Jim Kramer.

- They will have listened to and read the words of successful investors like Warren Buffett and Donald Trump.

In short, they will have done everything, exercised every diligence a reasonable person might seek in order to avoid failure; but too many will have failed anyway.

The real reason people either fail outright, or fail to succeed to the degree they might have desired - are *these* very sources and the "information" they spew. The entire body of conventional wisdom shapes what we think and how we behave when it comes to money. And I contend it is incomplete at best - self-serving at worst.

Playing the wealth building game is like playing Blackjack in Vegas. Sure there are winners - sometimes big, spectacular winners - witnessed by gathering crowds - urging others on with cheers of encouragement. But when the casino empties out the bins beneath the slot in the top of the table that all the cash is stuffed through - the house always comes out on top.

That's how I view conventional financial wisdom - it's not that it's bad - or intentionally misleading. And I certainly don't mean to imply that there is anything dishonest, sinister, or sleazy about the mainstreamers - particularly the ones you work with locally. They didn't make the rules. They're like the blackjack dealer; friendly, even rooting you on - pulling for you to "put one over on the house." They're playing by the rules they've been given - but their role in your outcome - despite what we may want to believe - is more a matter of chance than some double-top-secret advantage they may have been able to swing your way.

When we do win - and toss that dealer a $50 chip (as if they really played a role in our victory) - that's the equivalent of the big Wall Street brokers taking home those $5 million bonuses we read about each year.

When I was a kid - my brother had a go-cart. The engine had a governor on it. Dad told us the role of the governor was to keep the engine from running too fast and conking out. We knew better of course - its real role was to keep the go-cart from reaching maximum speed - giving Dad a little peace of mind in the process.

But we were more interested in speed than the longevity of the engine. So we learned to drive with one hand, while reaching behind us to the motor, to push the throttle past the point where the governor would limit the engine's output. It was much more fun that way. Sound familiar?

I believe Conventional wisdom is like a governor on our wealth building engine. If I didn't know it was there - or if I didn't know how to override it - I might achieve some level of financial success and never be the wiser. I might be perfectly content with my outcome - oblivious to the possibility that I might have done even better were it not for the invisible, but outcome-limiting drag of conventional wisdom.

In this book, I want to show you that conventional wisdom is like a governor on your wealth; and I want to give you a chance to take the governor off of your wealth building engine. And in the world of building a personal financial fortune, I believe you'll discover that taking the governor off means we can reach our destination in good stead, by an easier - less treacherous path that offers more predictability and in all likelihood, a better ultimate outcome. And the bonus is that we won't ruin the engine doing so - Dad!

Now I know I'm treading on sacred ground and riling the feathers of those who live in and rely on conventional wisdom. But I'm going to take on the mainstream financial industry - not the individuals - the institutions. Nonetheless, this journey will land me squarely in the company of the masked magician in the recent TV series, Magic's Secrets - Revealed.

In spilling some of the industry secrets, I may win fans among my readership, but missing among them will be my colleagues in the financial advisory community - including several close personal friends. I don't intend to attack them - just the casino and casino rules they play in and by. Remember, they're just the blackjack dealer - doing the best they can within the rule set they've been handed. They're not the bad guys here. Perhaps it would be a good time to borrow the words of another contrarian financial thinker who puts this all in much more eloquent words:

> *"There are two kinds of investors, be they large or small; those who don't know where the market is headed, and those who don't know that they don't know. Then again - there is a third type of investor - the investment professional, who indeed knows that he or she doesn't know, but whose livelihood depends upon appearing to know."*
>
> William Bernstein, The Intelligent Asset Allocator (New York: McGraw-Hill, 2001)

My invitation to you is this. Suspend - at least temporarily - what you believe and what you have been taught about money, finances, and investing. Allow for the possibility that there might be another way to "skin the cat." Follow the lead of the Queen of Spain who, had she - like all the others - dismissed Christopher Columbus as a kook, may have unwittingly allowed the Flat-Earth Society to rule to this day, leaving the New World, undiscovered.

While my vanity stops short of likening the journey you're about to take with me to discovering the New World, there may in fact be a new world of financial wisdom - and maybe - just maybe - a few morsels are shallowly buried beneath the pages that lie before you.

In the end, you'll be the judge of my logic. If you think I'm wrong after an objective evaluation, I'll accept your conclusion and wish you the greatest possible financial success. But if some of what I have to say causes an uncomfortable knot in your stomach to churn a bit - my words just might be validating an instinct that's been festering for a long time - but that has gone unspoken and undeclared for lack of a better answer. I hope you find some of those answers here.

Part I - Setting the Stage

"Conventional Wisdom is often...Neither"
Chinese Fortune Cookie

Chapter 1

Discovering your "Why?"

Chances are, you've become good at something and someone is paying you to do what you're good at. You're an administrator, a tradesman, a teacher, an entrepreneur, a professional, a business owner, a public servant, whatever. You've developed a skill set and you apply that skill in such a way that it generates a paycheck that supports you and your family. You've fulfilled the first requirement of wealth building.

But as good as you are at what you do - as much money as your skill commands - you can't claim financial victory yet. In fact, you're only halfway there. Because making money is only half the job. The other half is setting some of it aside and making it do what you want it to do - grow up to be what you want it to be - and that skill set is entirely different. It is unnatural - it is a foreign language - and it requires a personal discipline that can be elusive.

But we do it anyway - rarely asking why. For most red-blooded Americans, the "why" may seem obvious. But my belief is that motivation drives strategy. In other words, the *why* influences the *how* - so it bears a bit of discussion. Here are the three reasons most of us get into the game.

1. **Security**. As we mature, we take on a great deal of financial responsibility. Perhaps we take on the responsibility of a spouse, or children, or – as is becoming the case more and more – aging parents. Most of those responsibilities are of long-term duration. All of them require money. And the acquisition, preservation, care, and feeding...of money becomes a pursuit of both supreme importance and utmost urgency.

2. **Stuff**. We all want to increase our standard of living. We want to get out of that apartment and into a house. We want to buy a new car – or at least a newer car. We want to have more *money* than *month* for a change. We want to send our kids to college without debt. We want to travel, retire at a reasonable age, enjoy the finer things in life, and so on.

Increasing our standard of living is how we're wired, it's not greed – most of the time it is not selfish - it is perfectly natural and it's one of the things that sets us apart as Americans. Aspiring for a better life for our families and ourselves is, by most measures, a noble pursuit.

3. **People**. Many of us are very outward-focused, and see unquenchable need in the world that surrounds us. For us, the motivation to acquire and grow our financial resources is a means to helping meet the needs of those who can't quite get there by their own means. As humans, we're made in the image of God –the greatest model of a giver imaginable. Giving provides purpose and meaning to our lives - it represents work that is of enduring and eternal value – and therefore is important and relevant.

Your "Why" may be different. It may be a compilation of these and others. In the end, whatever your motivation - it is exclusively yours. It is personal and it is important. It's the stuff that gets us out of bed in the morning. Embrace your "Why." Remind yourself of it. Keep it in the front of your mind. And do everything you can to satisfy it - including of course - giving careful attention to the words that lie in front of you.

Chapter 2

How to Fail

As you think about your "Why" the realities of the wealth building task can seem daunting - overwhelming. Where to start? How to map out a game plan? Where to collect information? Who to listen to and who to trust?

Clearly, winning the financial game is the big elephant in the room. But as a wise man once said - the best way to eat an elephant - is one bite at a time. So let's break the task of building wealth into bite-sized chunks - starting with the two potential outcomes of our effort.

- We can win the Wealth Building game
- We can lose the Wealth Building game.

And that brings us to my first point of departure from mainstream financial wisdom. I believe it's more important to start our discussion not by figuring out how to win - but by figuring how *not to lose*. Fortunately when we break it all down to simple common denominators, there are only three ways we can fail in the money game. I call them the ***Three Failure Traps***:

Failure Trap No. One: Don't save and invest in the first place.

Failure Trap No. Two: Put money into things that (can) lose value.

Failure Trap No. Three: Die before the job is done.

Perhaps even more fortunately, all three failure traps are *completely avoidable* - yes - even failure trap number three (well, maybe not the death part, but certainly the financial consequences of death).

Only when we've learned how to tame the failure traps should we turn our focus to the offensive component of our success formula. By taking failure out of the equation, we can begin to sleep better - and by plotting a course toward guaranteed success - we can begin to dream more *while* we're sleeping. How about that - a financial cure for insomnia, poor sleep, and unsatisfying dreams?

Unlike most mainstreamers, I will not start a conversation about wealth building by talking about offense - what kinds of things we'll do to grow money. Offense may be more fun - it may endear me to more readers and clients alike - but compared to avoiding the three failure traps, *it is the least important of the wealth building variables*.

So back to the failure traps.

I'm not going to use the space in this book to talk about failure trap number one, *"fail to save and invest in the first place."* I'll leave that to other books, parents, professors, and pundits. Instead, I'm going to assume you already have that part of the equation figured out. Suffice to say that the first failure trap is totally up to you - not me; and I don't believe you would have read even this far if you weren't adequately motivated and committed to succeed.

The bulk of our time will be spent exploring Failure Trap No. Two - *putting money into things that can, and often do - lose value.* As you'll see a bit later, there are only three ways to lose money - three boogey men that loom out there in investing-land. If we can avoid them or tame them - I promise you'll be miles ahead of everybody else on your block - right out of the gate. Their names are Risk - Taxes - and Fees. More on them - much more - later.

But let's talk about *Failure Trap No. Three* for a moment. While none of us knows or controls the day we'll get our "final promotion" as a good friend puts it - there is one sure-fire way to avoid the financial consequences of dying before we've secured our family's financial future - and it's called life insurance. It is inexpensive - it's certain - and for some reason, it's reviled - all at the same time. You don't have to like life insurance – but you do have to own some.

You wouldn't buy a house and not insure it. You wouldn't drive a car without automobile insurance. Yet those are just our golden eggs. What we need to insure is the golden goose - the one that produces the golden eggs - and that's a living, breathing - YOU!

Sometimes the Golden Goose dies. Life insurance allows the Golden Goose - even in its dead state - to keep producing golden eggs for our families. All the financial obligations and aspirations you have for those you love and have taken responsibility for can be met even if you're not here to complete the job yourself, with simple, inexpensive life insurance.

4

Later in this book, we'll talk more about life insurance (I know – you can't wait). But for now, all you need to know is that you must have some. Choose to ignore this step, and getting the others right might not matter.

Consider this: you could live on beans and rice; save 80% of every nickel you make; achieve investment returns of 100% per year - but if you only have until tomorrow on this earth, it will all be for naught. You will have sacrificed lifestyle today, for a tomorrow that never comes. What's worse - those you leave behind will not only have to carry on without you, but they'll likely be left with insufficient financial means of doing so. End of lecture - get over it - and be sure you're adequately insured.

Rigged

Chapter 3

Rules of Engagement

If we pay serious attention to the failure traps in the last chapter, then we're well on our way to achieving my first immutable rule of investing:

Rule No. One: Failure is NOT an option

What exactly does that mean? It means that the business of building wealth is serious stuff - so serious in fact that we simply cannot fail - we must resolve not to fail.

All of us know someone who is retired without the financial resources to do so comfortably. That's very sad. For the most part these are people who have worked hard their whole lives. They're people who - at one time anyway - had dreams of a reasonably comfortable retirement. Now - they're shut-ins and Wal-Mart greeters. And we ask ourselves why? How can such things happen in this country?

Some were unlucky. Some were reckless. Some relied too much on the safety net of Social Security. When you encounter these people, I hope you'll turn that sadness into a personal resolve not to fail yourself. How hopeless people must feel when they wake up at 70 years of age with little in the bank - watching out the window for the mailman to deliver this month's social security check.

While we're on the subject, a word about social security. Today, Social Security represents about 38% of the income of the average retiree. That's already way too high given the original intent of Social Security, but there are two trends that make that statistic truly alarming.

First, that 38% figure was just 30% in 1962. In other words, social security makes up 1/3 more of the income of today's average retiree - than it did 50 years ago. Why? There are three primary reasons.

For one, there are fewer traditional pensions to make up the difference. How many people do you know under the age of 60 who have a traditional pension - guaranteed retirement income? Probably very few. Now, how many of you grew up in a household with parents who benefitted from a traditional pension?

This is generally not the case now as traditional pensions have gone the way of the dinosaur. The simple fact is that pensions are expensive to offer, and since the advent of the qualified plan in the '70's, the responsibility for retirement income has shifted almost completely from the employer (the traditional pension) to the employee (good luck - you're on your own).

And that leads to the second reason. Roller coaster investment markets and financial ignorance have not positioned people to pick up the ball and successfully carry it to the finish line themselves. As we said before, putting money to work requires a completely different skill set than earning it in the first place. And just as most of us will never learn how to fix the furnace, we generally don't have time or patience to acquire the knowledge to build wealth effectively and with the best possible outcome. Like the furnace - we outsource it instead.

Too many people invest more time in knowing what the latest celebrity *du jour* is up to than they do learning how to secure their financial future. Your investment in this book distinguishes you as the exception to that rule.

Third, too many people just don't have the discipline to save and keep their hands off their money. Some will save it ... until the first emergency, the latest iPhone, or new-fangled flat screen comes along. The saving discipline is something we're not very good at as a rule, but is THE critical practice for wealth-builders.

The other alarming trend about social security is that for two-thirds of American retirees, social security will account for more than half of their total retirement income; and for one-third of them, it will make up more than 90% of their total income.

With Social Security being so critically important to so many - maybe we should know what the future of that program looks like. Below is the *exact language* that is printed on the front page of the annual social security statement each of us receives each year. From the Social Security Administration:

> **"In 2016, we will begin paying more in benefits than we collect in taxes. Without changes, by 2037 the Social Security Trust Fund will**

be exhausted and there will be enough money to pay only about 76 cents for each dollar of scheduled benefits. We need to resolve these issues soon to make sure Social Security continues to provide a foundation of protection for future generations."

Michael J. Astrue, Commissioner

Would it be fair to read this language as a warning - or a "pre-apology" for the absence of benefits when we get to retirement? Perhaps. But regardless, it puts more pressure on us to rely on ourselves, rather than on others when it comes to our retirement income and lifestyle.

As if that's not frightening enough, let's look at where the *rest* of Americans' retirement income comes from. According to a 2008 study (*before* the big 2008 stock market crash), 29% came from "earned income" - in other words - wages from working in retirement. Nine percent comes from pensions; and 11% comes from assets - meaning the personal wealth people have built that we're talking about in this book.

Social Security	38%
Work	29%
Pensions	9%
Assets	11%

Considering these categories, here's my question. Which of these do you and I control - and which ones are outside our ability to control?

We don't control social security - heck - based on Astrue's warning above - we can't even build a convincing case that it will be there for us. We don't control our ability to work and earn income - health and job availability issues largely determine that. And do you have a guaranteed lifetime pension anymore?

The "Asset" category is the only one we can truly control - what kind of collection of financial assets we build on our own is the only element of our retirement income we have the ability to influence or control.

As if Rule Number One: ***Failure is Not an Option*** - needed any more reinforcement, you should now have all the evidence you need to get very serious about the task in front of you.

So let's assume that you take the failure traps seriously. You are saving and investing with a vengeance - so **Failure Trap No. 1** - ***Don't Save and***

Invest in the First Place - is checked off the list. And, you have good and adequate life insurance in place, so **Failure Trap No. 3** - *Die before the job is done* - is also sufficiently neutralized.

Now, you will only have to avoid **Failure Trap No. 2** - *Make Investment Decisions that Lose Money* - in order to not fail (we'll talk about succeeding later). Avoiding investment decisions that lose money is a tough one – but it's so critically important that my second rule of investing is:

Rule No. Two: First, Lose No Money!

I borrowed rule number two from two sources. First, the Doctor's Hippocratic oath that says in part, "first, do no harm." Of all the admonitions and advice the medical profession dispenses to aspiring young medical students and the doctors it produces - why would they start with, "first, do no harm?"

I believe it is for the same reason that the rule applies to investing. Because the end game is so important - of such a critical nature - that any steps backward may prove irreversible and unsurvivable. It's always better to live with a limp, than to die by way of a failed cure. Dead is dead - and broke is broke.

I also borrowed rule number two from a guy named Warren Buffett - perhaps the greatest investor in American History - even world history. It's Buffett's rule number one. In fact, Buffett thinks it's so important that *his* rule number two is - ***refer to rule number one!*** I would go so far as to say that it would be <u>impossible to abide rule number one - ***Failure is Not an Option***</u> - without rule number two, ***First, Lose No Money***.

Chapter 4

Thinking Defense First

To build wealth, we need a game plan. And our game plan has an offensive component and a defensive component. The offensive component means deciding where we're going to put money (what kinds of instruments and investments), and why we're going to put it there (what do we expect of those investments). Our defensive game plan must consider how we're going to "lose no money." Both are important, but if we ignore or fail to prioritize defense first, the best offensive game plan on the planet may be of no help to us in the long run.

A wise man once said - the best way to retire with $1,000,000 - is to start out with $2,000,000. It makes the point clearly. When the boat is filling with water, plotting the course ahead will not get us to our destination until the hole in the boat is plugged and the leakage is stopped.

So as we did when we reduced the wealth building task to the three failure traps, lets apply some simplified logic to losing no money. The good news is that I believe there are only three threats to our money - three ways to lose money - three predators that are more than happy to steal from us every step of the way. Eliminate them, and we take enormous pressure off the offensive component of our game plan.

The bad news is that this is where conventional financial wisdom lets us down. To the extent mainstreamers give defense any attention at all, they provide few meaningful alternatives. But we're getting ahead of ourselves. Here are the three financial predators we need to focus on:

1. **Market-Imposed losses** - markets, securities, and investment instruments that can (and often do) go down in value,

2. **Taxes** - Taxes will steal a share of every penny of wealth we accumulate - if we let them,

3. **Investing Fees and Commissions** - The cost of investing fees act as a boat anchor on our earnings.

In later chapters, I'm going to show you exactly how we can eliminate these three from our wealth building equation. Before going there however, it's critical to understand just what significant parasites they are. Because while conventional financial wisdom may talk about managing risk - or managing our tax liability - they never really get serious about *eliminating* these three kinds of losses as the first goal in our quest for wealth.

Talking about losses means talking about defense. It's not sexy or fun. It doesn't put points on the board - and you'll never hear an investment advisor pitching you to use them based on their "crack defensive strategies." But when it comes to defense - think of it this way:

> *"Offense sells tickets, defense wins championships."*
> Bear Bryant, Alabama Football Coach

The "Bear" couldn't have put it better. Let me translate from football to wealth-building. In wealth building, *defense* [not losing money] wins *championships* [big fat retirement accounts], *offense* [investments with the potential for big returns], sells *tickets* [gets clients to "purchase" advice from high-priced advisors].

Our defensive financial game plan has sub-components - just like a football team needs separate strategies to stop the pass, the run, and special teams. If they do well at one but not the others - it may not matter.

The same applies to money. If we eliminate the possibility of investing losses from every transaction or trade we ever make, but ignore the predators of, taxes and investing fees/commissions, we may grow our wealth - but these two will gnaw away at our progress.

So if we don't neutralize all three simultaneously, we won't be fully attending the rule, and we'll sub-optimize our results in a significant way. Tame all three, and almost regardless of how good or not-so-good we do on the offensive side of the equation (investment picking), we will have done more to ensure that we build a personal fortune than anybody else on our block - in our office - in our church - or in our bowling league - combined!

Now when I say we have to **neutralize** investment risk, taxes, and investment costs, don't I really mean, "manage" these risks - everybody knows you can't get rid of them completely, right? Besides, do they really have as dramatic an effect on our outcome as I'm suggesting?

All reasonable questions and reactions. Conventional Wisdom-itis does that to us. In the following chapters I'll answer those questions. That's why Part II of this book will prove so important.

Rigged

Part II - The Big Three

"October is one of the peculiarly dangerous months to speculate in stocks. The others are July, January, September, April, November, May, March, June, December, August and February."

Mark Twain

Rigged

Chapter 5

The Devastation of Losses

In this case, the Big Three does not refer to Ford, Chrysler, and GM. For our purposes, the Big Three refers to what we just covered - the three ways of losing money: Investment Losses, Taxes, and Investing Fees and Commissions.

The first of these is *investing losses*. Now at first blush, it might seem there are a thousand ways to lose money - so many in fact that wealth building can seem like a February street - so full of potholes that the goal is to hit just a few - because avoiding them all is impossible.

Thankfully, I don't think it's quite that daunting. But we first have to get over the conventional view of losses - which is that they're "*part of the game*" - "*you can't win every time*" - "*if you're not taking a loss from time to time, you're really not in the game*" - "*occasional losses are the price we pay for big gains.*"

These may sound reasonable - *in the context of the conventional world*, but to me - they're rationalizations advanced by a mainstream financial community that has no more idea of how to immunize your portfolio from investing losses than the man in the moon.

Rationalizations aside - let's look at losses through new eyes. I'll start with two statements about investment losses that you may have never heard before.

1. Losses are *always more devastating* than we allow ourselves to believe.
2. Losses are *irrecoverable*. Our account balance might recover, but losses can never be recovered.

That's not my opinion - it's math - so let's look at each statement closely.

Losses are always more devastating than we allow ourselves to believe. Let's use a story problem to make the point. I know it's been a while since you did story problems, and you probably don't like them any better now than you did then, so I'll make it a multiple choice story problem.

> Jill has $100,000 in an investment account. Over the course of the next 10 years, her account grows by 7.2% each year - uninterrupted, doubling her account to exactly $200,000. Jack starts out with the same $100,000 in his investment account. His experience is the same as Jill's - with one exception. One year, Jack had a little setback where rather than his account growing by 7.2%; he actually suffers a small 5% loss. At the end of 10 years, how much *less* money does Jack have in his account, than Jill has in hers?
>
> > a. Jack has $1,400 less than Jill
> >
> > b. Jack has $3,750 less than Jill
> >
> > c. Jack has $8,750 less than Jill
> >
> > d. Jack has $17,150 less than Jill

Okay - I tricked you. The answer is "e" none of the above. Jack actually has $34,300 less - twice the highest of the answers. That means Jill's account is at $200,000; Jack's is at $165,700. Jill has 20.1% more money than Jack.

Wait a minute - I thought you said Jack had just a 5% loss in just one year. How does that translate to Jill ending up with 20.1% more money than Jack?

It's called compounding. When it works *for* you, it's magic. When it works *against* you, it's devastating. And here we see just how devastating - in a very simple example that we've probably all experienced - perhaps many times over - but may have never analyzed properly as we've done here.

How much do you hope to have in your wealth account when you retire? $1,000,000? $5,000,000? If, over the course of your investing life, you have *one little tiny 5% setback year*, then instead of $1,000,000, you'll have 20.1% less - $832,000. Instead of $5,000,000, you'll have $4,164,000.

Would that make a lifestyle difference in your world? Would it make a legacy difference? Hold on - it gets worse. Remember my second statement?

Losses are irrecoverable - What in the world do I mean by " irrecoverable?" I mean that we tend to shrug off losses as just *part of the game*, because more often than not, our account balance recovers. As it does, the pain of the loss fades into the past. What we fail to realize however, is that the scar tissue of the loss stays with us forever.

Let me demonstrate the irrecoverability of losses with another story problem that picks up with Jack and Jill right where we left off:

> In our last problem, Jill grew her investment account from $100,000 - to $200,000 in 10 years, and Jack grew his account from $100,000 to $165,700. If both Jack and Jill double their accounts over the next 10 years:
>
> | How much does Jill end up with? | $400,000 |
> |---|---|
> | How much does Jack end up with? | <u>$331,400</u> |
> | What's the difference? | $ 68,600 |
>
> How much more money does Jill have than Jack? 20.1% more!

See what I mean? *Jack never recovers the loss.* Jill will always have 20.1% more money than Jack even if their returns mirror each other for 10 years, 20 years, or 50 years. Losses can never be recovered.

Account balances can recover - but not losses. Jack's account balance recovered quite nicely. Turning $100,000 into $331,400 over 20 years is no small feat. But that little teeny tiny 5% setback that he suffered way back when - stays with him forever.

And herein lies one of the deceits of the mainstreamers. They want Jack to focus on his "success" at turning $100,000 into $331,400. In fact, they not only congratulate Jack, they congratulate themselves too. They don't want you to know, look at, calculate, or otherwise speculate on what could have been, had that loss never happened in the first place. They hope Jack never runs into Jill and the two of them start comparing notes.

- Has anyone - your parents, your teachers or professors, Dave Ramsey, the Wall Street Journal, your investment advisor - anyone - ever shown you the devastating impact of losses this way before?

- Does it make you feel a little differently about how seriously you take your defensive strategy?

- Does it leave you a little sick about the losses you may have sustained in the past?

- How likely is it that the market will have a 5% hiccup over any 10 year period of time?

- How many times - over the course of your investing lifetime - is the market likely to have a down year?

- Does the market ever go down by more than 5%?

- Is the market ever flat?

- Have you ever lost 5% or more on an investment?

Now you know what I mean when I make my two bold statements about investing losses:

1. Losses are always more devastating than we allow ourselves to believe.
2. Losses are not recoverable. Our account balance might recover, but losses never can be.

I hope this is beginning to change the way you look at the mainstream investing world.

Let's summarize what we've covered so far: We know there are three ways to fail - we know two of them can be disposed of relatively easily - and now we know that the big one - losing money - comes in just three forms - and we're going to deal with them with equally efficient dispatch.

Failure Trap	Antidote
1. Fail to Save and Invest	Just Do It!
2. Make Investments that Lose Money	a. Shift Market Risk Elsewhere
	b. Build Tax-Free Wealth
	c. Minimize Investing Costs
3. Die before the Job is Complete	Have adequate Life Insurance

Chapter 6
The Devastation Of Taxes

The good news about losses is that we can make a conscious decision to steer away from them. Within the spectrum of mainstream investment options, risk can be avoided today in the form of CD's, money market funds, stuffing it in the mattress, and a few others. Of course, those all come at the cost of anemic returns that won't get us to the finish line we dream of. Later, we'll talk about a way of eliminating (yes - eliminating, not minimizing) risk without giving up much, if any of the upside of the market returns we want.

Taxes - on the other hand, are largely viewed as completely inescapable. But the minute we accept that outcome - the minute we accept taxes as a matter-of-fact part of investing, we make an instantaneous and irreversible decision. We resign ourselves to taking a *silent partner* along with us on our lifetime wealth-building journey. His name is Uncle Sam. He brings absolutely nothing of value to the partnership - he just sits quietly - watching closely - cheering us on - knowing the day is coming when he can claim his share of the partnership without so much as a "thank you."

If he ever gets the notion that his share of the partnership is inadequate, he'll just increase it by making a change in the tax code. And unfortunately this partnership doesn't operate like other partnerships - where the partners discuss and decide on changes to the partnership agreement by mutual consent. In this one, he has complete dictatorial and unilateral control over his partnership share - leaving us no voice - no objection - no vote - no say - whatsoever.

So given that we have this partner we have to deal with, we're forced - by the mainstreamers - down one of two paths.

1. There's the *"pay-as-you-go"* path - also known as investing after-tax dollars; or
2. There's the *"pay-me-later"* path - also known as tax-qualified plans - perhaps better known by their more familiar names, the IRA, 401(k), Keogh, SIMPLE, SEP, and others.

Oh, there is one hybrid path - the Roth IRA - where we can invest after tax-dollars, but take our money out tax-free. The Roth can be a great option, but it's plagued by three problems. First, many of us don't qualify for a Roth IRA. Second, the contribution limits are such that they can really only serve as supplemental accounts - not primary wealth building accounts. And third, we're subject to a 10% penalty if we ever need to get at our money prior to retirement.

I don't want to ignore the Roth - in fact I'll introduce you to a Super-Roth later in this book - and share with you exactly what it is. I call it a Super-Roth because it eliminates all three of the limitations we just outlined. But for now, I want to focus on the two paths most of us choose - the taxable account path, and the qualified plan path.

The advantage of building wealth with after-tax dollars is that our money is accessible - we can get at it without penalty in a time of need or opportunity. The disadvantage is that we have substantially fewer dollars to invest after our money has been taxed. But if the purpose of saving and investing is for a pre-retirement need - like funding college, buying a home or car, or other needs, we have few choices other than to save and invest after-tax dollars.

Our other alternative is the tax-qualified plan (IRAs, 401(k)s, 403(b)s, SEPs, Keoghs, SIMPLE plans, and others). Started in the '70's, tax qualified plans were promoted by the government as a way to "put one over" on Uncle Sam by deferring taxes - making him wait for his money. Now let's be logical for a moment. Even if you bought that line - how many times do we really put one over on the government? Really?

Small businesses and entrepreneurs for example, feel particularly trapped by the pay-me-later method, because they often have emergencies and opportunities that require immediate access to their money. When it's locked away in a qualified plan of some kind, they might have to take $1.40 - or more - out of their plan, just to have $1.00 (after tax and penalty) to spend - a heavy price to pay for the privilege of deferring (not eliminating) taxes.

Nonetheless, qualified plans have collectively amassed a pretty good chunk of change over the years. According to the government, there is more than $14 trillion of personal wealth socked away in qualified plans – *all of which is subject to a tax rate that is unknown until it is taken out.*

Despite the fact that they only defer, rather than eliminate taxes, it's hard to argue that we should pay-as-we-go when we're given the pay-me-later option. The problem is that it's impossible to make an apples-to-apples comparison since we don't know - we can't know - what the tax rates will be tomorrow - and that's the trap they've laid.

Here's one thing we can say for sure. *Qualified Plans - in all their various iterations - will have the certain result that our tax bill will be as high as it can possibly be.*

The allure of qualified plans has been built on the proposition that if we defer our taxes into the future, our tax bracket will be lower in retirement than it is during our working years, because we'll be earning less. But that logic fails to recognize reality. While we're working and raising a family, we are able to access all sorts of deductions and credits that lower our effective tax rate - even if our gross income throws us into a relatively high tax bracket. In retirement, most of those deductions and credits are gone.

The lack of deductions means that while our tax bracket might be lower because our retirement income is lower, our *effective tax rate* may be higher and we end up paying more of our income in taxes in retirement than we did during our earning years. That's *if* tax rates are the same then as they are today. And that's the second part of the qualified plan tax trap.

Answer this question. Do you think tax rates will be higher, lower, or about the same - when you retire - compared to today? Statistically, more than 90% of you will say that tax rates will be higher in retirement. Now think about that - in this country we can hardly get 90% to agree that the sky is blue - but on this one - we have near unanimity. And we don't have to be brain surgeons to get behind that conclusion with conviction.

Consider the table below. These are the top marginal tax rates since the inception of the income tax in 1916.

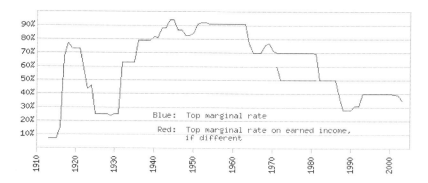

It wouldn't be hard to draw from this that today's tax rates are a relative bargain. For all but a short period of our history - in the late 1920's and early 1930's, tax rates have been higher than they are today. Hmm. What was going on in the late '20's and early '30's? And whose retirement are we really working for - ours - or the government's?

But that's history. What does the future hold? We need look little farther than into the country's present financial situation to cipher that one out.

- Our current national debt is approaching $17 trillion. That's $17,000,000,000,000 - and that's just what we've accumulated so far. Keep in mind, that figure is going up by about a trillion a year.

- Now beyond the $17 trillion, we've promised another $76 trillion to our citizens in the form of entitlements like social security and Medicare. Those liabilities are almost completely unfunded - meaning we're not saving money today so we can pay the bill tomorrow.

- Now the $76 trillion is only good if we assume two things. First, that our older citizens do us the favor of dying when they're supposed to so we can turn the spigot off. Second, since nearly every penny of the benefits we do pay will be borrowed (as is the $17 trillion we already carry on the books), the $76 trillion assumes government borrowing costs will be where they are today - at historic lows. What if interest rates resume their natural levels of even say as low as 5-6%? What happens to that figure? Today, the interest cost on the $17 trillion is already more than <u>$1 billion a day.</u>

But it's actually worse. The problem with people dying when they're supposed to is that we're not - we're living longer - much longer - than we were when we last updated our mortality tables (life expectancy) - in 1980. Women, for example, are adding nearly 1 month of life expectancy per year at our current pace of advances in medical technology, treatment, and diagnosis.

Many economists estimate that factoring some semblance of mortality and interest rate reality into the equation, our true debt is somewhere north of $100 trillion - a number we can't even begin to get our heads around.

But let's say they're wrong. Let's say the government number is right - our projected debt is really a mere $76 trillion. That figure alone is more than $1,000,000 per taxpayer today (remember, almost half of all American citizens pay no income taxes). Oh - and guess what. As baby-boomers age and die, there will be considerably fewer taxpayers in the future. Then there's one other little thing I forgot. That's just the federal debt. It doesn't include the states and municipalities. Thankfully they're in good shape...not!

We know all this instinctively - but the shock value is truly sobering. There is absolutely no way tax rates 10 - 20 - or 30 years from now will be anything but higher - much higher than they are today. That exposes qualified plan money to a liability that's unknown - other than we know it will be higher.

Sorry to be Debbie Downer - but we're not done. There's a second "gotcha." Let's say we foil Uncle Sam's plan by taking out of our qualified plan only what we're absolutely required to take out (and pay taxes on) for the rest of our lives. That's called " required minimum distributions - or RMD's." We reach the end of our life, warmed by the knowledge that we're passing on what has ballooned to $5,000,000 in our qualified IRA account, and our kids and grandkids will want for little for generations to come.

Now remember, not a penny of that $5,000,000 has been taxed. If we die before our spouse, they'll be able to inherit the money without a tax - but when the spouse passes away, Uncle Sam goes to town like a buzzard on road kill.

The IRA money that passes on will be considered ordinary income to the recipient(s), so each beneficiary will be taxed on their own income plus that portion of their inheritance - and the tax will be due in the year of your death. The combination will put most heirs into a higher tax bracket - meaning not only will the inherited IRA money be heavily taxed - their regular income will be taxed at that same - higher - rate.

But wait, there's more!

Estate taxes, also known as death taxes - continue to be hotly debated. As of this writing, estate taxes are rather tame. But again if we use history to predict the future, they're likely to resurface with a vengeance. Consider what happens if the exemption threshold were to revert to $1,000,000 (as it has in the past). Someone dies with a $2.5 million estate - none of which is qualified money. Think that's a huge estate? Consider this: Someone who has accumulated $500,000 in taxable investments, a $600,000 primary residence, a $250,000 condo in Florida, $150,000 in other personal property, and a $1,000,000 life insurance policy. Total estate: $2.5 million (see how quickly it adds up)?

Estate Tax:

Gross estate	$2,500,000
Exemption	$1,000,000
Taxable Estate	$1,500,000
Federal Estate Tax	X 50%
Estate Tax	($750,000)
Net after Estate Tax	$1,750,000

Sorry - not done yet. Inheritance taxes are the state's version of the Federal Estate Tax. Most have some. Let's take Pennsylvania for example - and apply the lowest inheritance tax they assess.

Inheritance Tax

Gross Inheritance	$2,500,000
Inheritance Tax (4.5%)	$112,500
Net Estate after all Death Taxes	**$1,237,500**

While it may be hard to feel too sorry for someone inheriting over $1 million, consider the outcome from the point of view of the person leaving the estate. That $2.5 million estate represents their life's financial work – saving – investing – doing without – etc. Do you think it was their plan to share half of that with the government?

The simple fact is that taxes - in their entirety - are, and will continue to be, the greatest eroder of wealth on the planet. If we can eliminate them altogether, we'll be 30-50% ahead of the rest of the pack. That takes a huge amount of pressure off our offensive game plan, because without a tax obligation, we'll own every penny of that figure on our statement balance, and won't have to worry about the impact of future taxes.

Rigged

Chapter 7

The Devastation of Fees and Commissions

When we buy a bag of groceries or a new television, we generally don't think about sales tax - we just buy what we need and the tax is the tax. It's not something that dissuades us from making the purchase, nor is it generally something that makes us look for a tax-free way of buying goods and services.

And if sales tax at 5-10% won't change our purchasing habits, it's no wonder we tend not to pay much attention to fees and commissions either - since they generally consume only 2-4% of our account value.

But the truth is - this should be the center of our focus - and here's why. While income taxes apply only to the "gains" in our wealth account, fees and commissions apply to the whole thing - 100% of our money - and many of those fees and commissions are charged year in and year out.

Let me start with a question. How much did you pay per gallon the last time you filled up your car? I'll bet you know. You may even have driven a few extra blocks because one gas station was selling gas $.02/gallon cheaper than one that was closer to your home or office. So let's see - we'll drive out of our way to save $.30 on a fill-up, but we don't know how much is leaking from our investment accounts in fees and commissions? Does that make any sense at all?

You may recall how shocking it was to learn in: *The Devastation of Losses* chapter, that a little 5% down year in a whole string of up years, cost us an unrecoverable 20.1% in our ending account balance. Well - brace yourself. Investing fees - in all their various forms and fashions, have a huge cumulative effect. They don't seem that harmful at the time; "What's the big deal about a few percentage points in fees for all the professional advice I get?" So let's look.

Jill gets serious about saving and investing starting at age 35. She puts $1,000/month into an investment account with one of the big Wall Street brokerage firms her friend works at. For this discussion, it doesn't matter if the account is taxable, or tax qualified.

She's pretty good with spreadsheets, so she estimated what her money would grow to by the time she retires at age 65. She's optimistic - so she figures she can earn 10% on her money on average. Her spreadsheet tells her that by 65, she will have invested $360,000 of her own money (30 years x $12,000/year); and at 10% compounded; her money will grow to a whopping **$2,401,653**. Wow - she can almost feel the sand between her toes.

That is - until her friend Jack reminds her that she's made no provision for investment fees and commissions. He suggests she change the "return" from 10% to 9%. Surely that will give her an idea of the impact of fees - assuming they're about 1% per year, right?

She changes the spreadsheet and hits the "recalculate" button - more than a little anxious. Neither she nor Jack can believe their eyes. "There must be a mistake in the spreadsheet," Jack says - trying his hardest to keep Jill from passing out. But after a thorough check of the math, the numbers don't lie. Jill's new projected account balance - $1,917,044. How can it be? What happened to her $2,401,653? At just 1%, can her investment fees really add up to $484,609? That's a full 20.2% less money just because of fees.

Sure her broker-friend drives a nice car - lives in a nice home - takes regular vacations - but to think that Jill could pay nearly a half a million dollars during her accumulation years nearly makes her nauseous. Jill also realizes that the meter doesn't stop running at retirement - it will continue for the rest of her life - and could easily top $1,000,000.

Not even recovered from that reality, another wave of panic washes over her. She really never discussed fees with her broker - she just assumed they were reasonable and customary - but she has no idea whether they're 1% - or 5%? What if 1% is too low?

So she does a little internet research and finds a recently published white paper suggesting that fees and commissions - in all their various forms, can be as high as 4.44%; and for qualified plan owners, they regularly average 3.41%. Afraid to look, Jill plugs 3.41% into her spreadsheet and instantaneously, instead of $2.4 million, she is left with $1.1 million. That's 54% for the financial advisory industry, 46% for her.

Here's another shocking way to look at fees. If Jill starts her saving regimen by putting $1000 into her account, never adds another dime, and grows her money by 10% per annum - in 30 years, that original $1,000 grows to $19,000 with no fees or commissions. But if she paid just 2% in fees and commissions over that same 30 years, she ends up with just $7,500.

That means, that to deposit, warehouse and manage that initial $1,000, Jill will pay her broker $11,500 in fees and commissions. It's almost more than her mind can process. Sadly, it's all true. And now you know how Wall Street lives the way it does and hands out the bonuses it does.

In fact, "hide the fees" became such "sport" on Wall Street, that in 2012, legislators mandated that fees and commissions be completely disclosed. Wall Street fought the initiative tooth and nail, but it's here nonetheless. And the ugly truth is that those of you who are saving your money in qualified plans like IRAs, 401(k)s and others, are paying much more in fees than are those who are building wealth in a taxable account. Why? Because without these new disclosure laws, they could get away with financial murder.

Just ask yourself when was the last time you saw an investment advisor in a frayed suit, driving a 5-year old Chevy, in a strip center office. Perhaps now you know why. In fact, they're a lot like the TV weatherman. They can get it wrong - a lot - and still earn a pretty comfortable living.

Still not convinced? Let me offer a third-party perspective on the whole fees and commissions subject. Read this article from the Motley Fool - a financial information organization who has studied the issue:

Hidden 401(k) Fees: The Great Retirement Plan Rip-Off

By Adam J. Wiederman, The Motley Fool

You've been advised to save for retirement using your company's 401(k) plan. The benefits, after all, are significant:

1. Contributions are made with pre-tax dollars, lowering your taxable income each year you contribute.

2. The money you contribute, along with earnings, continues to grow tax-free until you begin to   withdraw.

3. Most plans include a matching contribution from your employer, handing you free money as an incentive to save.

Yet despite all these perks, a new study by Demos, a nonpartisan public policy research and advocacy organization, alleges that your 401(k) plan may be ripping you off in ways you don't even recognize.

What's worse, the typical 401(k) will steal an average of nearly $155,000 from each worker over a lifetime of saving.

'Secret' Fees Savers Don't Know They're Paying

The reason for this massive loss of wealth over a lifetime of saving comes down to fees. And those fees are usually expressed in a way that disguises the true cost.

Most investors who purchase mutual funds have heard of fees like the "expense ratio," which averages more than 1% annually. Funds in 401(k)s are not exempt from such fees, which cover the cost of record keeping and compliance, the fund manager's salary, and (sometimes) marketing fees.

While the expense ratio is publicly shared, there are other fees that, Demos found, "are nearly completely hidden from retirement savers." We're talking about "trading fees."

Trading fees are costs incurred when a mutual fund buys or sells an investment, in the form of commissions and bid/ask spreads (the difference between the price the fund actually buys or sells it for versus its market value). And they vary based on how actively a mutual fund is trading.

But good luck trying to figure out how much you're actually paying for trading fees.

Obscure Reporting at Its Finest

The biggest problem facing 401(k) sleuths is that "reporting fees as a percentage of assets actually disguises their true cost," according to the Demos report.

Demos compares it to receiving a surcharge on a concert ticket purchase. Let's say you buy a ticket to a show. The ticket company bases its fee on the price of the ticket. So, for example, if the fee is 5%, you pay 5% of the price of the value of the good they're selling you.

Mutual funds, on the other hand, charge customers a fixed amount based on your account balance, not a percentage of the returns they earned on your money (which is the value they actually provided). It's akin to paying 5% of your bank account balance to the ticket seller in order to buy admission to the show.

In other words, mutual funds that employ this practice are paid even if they just hold onto your money. They don't have nearly as much incentive to actually earn returns on your money because *they get paid no matter what*.

You Only Think You're Paying 1.23% in Fees...

The study shares an example fund in which a $50,000 investment earned 4.65% net. Meaning after one year, the account was worth $52,325.

In reality, of course, the fund earned more on that initial $50,000. The stated expense ratio was 1.23%, so $615 in fees came out prior to that return. That means the fund actually made $2,930 gross, or 5.88% of the initial $50,000.

However, the study encourages us to look at this in another way -- by expressing fees as a percentage of the gross return. To do this, take the $615 in fees, and divide it by the gross return of $2,930. This equates to a startling 20.9% of its return in fees -- meaning an investor paid 20.9% of the value the fund added.

But this still doesn't take into consideration those obscure "trading fees" mentioned above. According to Demos, trading fees "often cost savers as much as or more than the explicit expense ratio," meaning this example fund probably had a "real expense ratio" of 2.46%.

Since trading fees come out of the gross returns, we can adjust the fund's gross (pre-fee) return to 7.11%. Meaning the fund actually earned $3,555 before fees. It gets worse.

... You're Actually Shelling Out More Than 30%

Combining the expense ratio and trading fees, this fund withdrew $1,230 in fees ($615 + $615). Dividing this by the gross return of $3,555, an investor in this fund paid a startling 34.6% in "true fees."

In other words, an investor paid a whopping $1,230 for $2,325 to be made on his money.

Add this up over a lifetime of saving and investing in a 401(k) plan and the average worker loses as much as $154,794, according to Demos. A higher-income household can expect to lose even more -- as much as $277,969.

As Demos' study sums up, "Considering that a significant portion of these fees goes to paying the high salaries and expenses of the investment professionals managing these funds, asking struggling

American households to pay these prices to save for retirement is more than patently unfair, it's immoral."

Unfortunately, the options for investors who want to avoid the fee frenzy are limited.

Stuck With a Rigged System?

One way around the fee issue is to take charge of your saving yourself, investing in a self-directed brokerage account through your company's 401(k) plan. Or you could make use of IRAs or taxable accounts.

The trade-off is that you lose some of the biggest perks of a 401(k) -- either a company match, or tax-free growth. After all, it's necessary to save for your own retirement. And a 401(k) is still the most tax-efficient way to save for retirement.

But the system is clearly broken. So until the 401(k) system gets fixed, it's a lose-lose situation for all too many investors.

Motley Fool analyst Adam J. Wiederman wrote this article.

The only issue I take with the author is that we're not stuck with a Rigged system - that's why you bought this book - and I promise, you will learn a different way.

Chapter 8

Losses + Taxes + Fees and Commissions

If you've peeked at the pages that follow, you've noticed a bunch of numbers - and if you're not the numbers kind, you may be tempted to skip this chapter. Please don't. I'll do my part not to overcomplicate this, but if the picture I'm about to paint in this chapter doesn't crystallize in your brain, the rest of this book will not make much sense to you either.

For the last few chapters, we've been talking about defense - figuring out how to not lose money before we take on how to make money. We've said that there are only three ways to lose money:

1. Invest in things that involve risk to principal and can go down in value
2. Invest in accounts and instruments that are subject to income and other taxes, and
3. Invest in things and accounts that come with fees, commissions, and other costs.

We looked at each separately, and I hope you gained some new perspective on these subjects. In this chapter, I want to put it all together in order to show you - in dramatic fashion - why I'm such an advocate of Defense First.

What we've just been through should have been the first thing you were taught by anyone who truly has your best financial interest in mind. But it's not. In fact, for many of you to whom this is new information, it's never been shared with you. But it's critically important - and you're about to see why.

We're going to revisit Jill from the last chapter - who commits to saving $1,000/month and investing it at 10% per annum, until retirement. Let's start with a baseline.

Rigged

						0.0%	0%	
Age	Yr	Beg Bal	Savings	Growth %	Growth $	Fees	Taxes	End Bal
35	1	0	12,000	10%	1,200	0	0	13,200
36	2	13,200	12,000	10%	2,520	0	0	27,720
37	3	27,720	12,000	10%	3,972	0	0	43,692
38	4	43,692	12,000	10%	5,569	0	0	61,261
39	5	61,261	12,000	10%	7,326	0	0	80,587
40	6	80,587	12,000	10%	9,259	0	0	101,846
41	7	101,846	12,000	10%	11,385	0	0	125,231
42	8	125,231	12,000	10%	13,723	0	0	150,954
43	9	150,954	12,000	10%	16,295	0	0	179,249
44	10	179,249	12,000	10%	19,125	0	0	210,374
45	11	210,374	12,000	10%	22,237	0	0	244,611
46	12	244,611	12,000	10%	25,661	0	0	282,273
47	13	282,273	12,000	10%	29,427	0	0	323,700
48	14	323,700	12,000	10%	33,570	0	0	369,270
49	15	369,270	12,000	10%	38,127	0	0	419,397
50	16	419,397	12,000	10%	43,140	0	0	474,536
51	17	474,536	12,000	10%	48,654	0	0	535,190
52	18	535,190	12,000	10%	54,719	0	0	601,909
53	19	601,909	12,000	10%	61,391	0	0	675,300
54	20	675,300	12,000	10%	68,730	0	0	756,030
55	21	756,030	12,000	10%	76,803	0	0	844,833
56	22	844,833	12,000	10%	85,683	0	0	942,516
57	23	942,516	12,000	10%	95,452	0	0	1,049,968
58	24	1,049,968	12,000	10%	106,197	0	0	1,168,165
59	25	1,168,165	12,000	10%	118,016	0	0	1,298,181
60	26	1,298,181	12,000	10%	131,018	0	0	1,441,199
61	27	1,441,199	12,000	10%	145,320	0	0	1,598,519
62	28	1,598,519	12,000	10%	161,052	0	0	1,771,571
63	29	1,771,571	12,000	10%	178,357	0	0	1,961,928
64	30	1,961,928	12,000	10%	197,393	0	0	2,171,321
65	31	2,171,321	12,000	10%	218,332	0	0	**2,401,653**

The table above shows the straight math of saving $12,000 per year
($1,000/month) beginning at age 35, and continuing through age 65.
We grow and compound those deposits at 10% per year uninterrupted,

and unburdened by investment losses, investing fees, or taxes. So our baseline figure shows that without those burdens, Jill would end up with $2,401,653.

Next, we introduce a minimum degree of market risk to the equation.

| | | | | | | 0.0% | 0% | |
Age	Year	Beg Bal	Savings	Growth %	Growth $$	Fees	Taxes	End Bal
35	1	0	12,000	10%	1,200	0	0	13,200
36	2	13,200	12,000	10%	2,520	0	0	27,720
37	3	27,720	12,000	10%	3,972	0	0	43,692
38	4	43,692	12,000	10%	5,569	0	0	61,261
39	5	61,261	12,000	5%	3,663	0	0	76,924
40	6	76,924	12,000	10%	8,892	0	0	97,817
41	7	97,817	12,000	10%	10,982	0	0	120,798
42	8	120,798	12,000	10%	13,280	0	0	146,078
43	9	146,078	12,000	10%	15,808	0	0	173,886
44	10	173,886	12,000	10%	18,589	0	0	204,475
45	11	204,475	12,000	10%	21,647	0	0	238,122
46	12	238,122	12,000	10%	25,012	0	0	275,134
47	13	275,134	12,000	10%	28,713	0	0	315,848
48	14	315,848	12,000	0%	0	0	0	327,848
49	15	327,848	12,000	10%	33,985	0	0	373,832
50	16	373,832	12,000	10%	38,583	0	0	424,416
51	17	424,416	12,000	10%	43,642	0	0	480,057
52	18	480,057	12,000	10%	49,206	0	0	541,263
53	19	541,263	12,000	10%	55,326	0	0	608,589
54	20	608,589	12,000	10%	62,059	0	0	682,648
55	21	682,648	12,000	10%	69,465	0	0	764,113
56	22	764,113	12,000	-5%	(38,806)	0	0	737,307
57	23	737,307	12,000	10%	74,931	0	0	824,238
58	24	824,238	12,000	10%	83,624	0	0	919,862
59	25	919,862	12,000	10%	93,186	0	0	1,025,048
60	26	1,025,048	12,000	10%	103,705	0	0	1,140,753
61	27	1,140,753	12,000	10%	115,275	0	0	1,268,028

62	28	1,268,028	12,000	10%	128,003	0	0	1,408,031
63	29	1,408,031	12,000	10%	142,003	0	0	1,562,034
64	30	1,562,034	12,000	10%	157,403	0	0	1,731,438
65	31	1,731,438	12,000	10%	174,344	0	0	**1,917,781**

In this table, I've interrupted the unbroken string of 10% gains in the three shaded years.

- In year 5, instead of a 10% gain, we have a 5% gain.
- Year 14 is flat - Jill's account neither gains nor loses ground.
- And year 22 is the one stinker in the whole 30-year time period where Jill suffers a 10% decline.

Note that I've only used one year where there is an actual loss, even though the market - statistically imposes losses on us 3 out of every 10 years. Note too that I've only introduced three years that break the 10% winning streak - pretty generous given the market's typical gyrations.

What impact did we have on Jill's bottom line? She went from $2,401,653 - to $1,917,781; a reduction of $483,872 - or 20.1%. That's 20% less money for Jill - nearly half a million less in retirement, from just one down year in 30 - something that's never happened in the recorded history of the stock market.

Next, let's take fees and commissions from Jill's account.

| | | | | | | 1.5% | 0% | |
Age	Year	Beg Bal	Savings	Growth %	Growth $$	Fees	Taxes	End Bal
35	1	0	12,000	10%	1,200	198	0	13,002
36	2	13,002	12,000	10%	2,500	413	0	27,090
37	3	27,090	12,000	10%	3,909	645	0	42,354
38	4	42,354	12,000	10%	5,435	897	0	58,892
39	5	58,892	12,000	5%	3,545	1,117	0	73,320
40	6	73,320	12,000	10%	8,532	1,408	0	92,444
41	7	92,444	12,000	10%	10,444	1,723	0	113,166
42	8	113,166	12,000	10%	12,517	2,065	0	135,617
43	9	135,617	12,000	10%	14,762	2,436	0	159,943

44	10	159,943	12,000	10%	17,194	2,837	0	186,300
45	11	186,300	12,000	10%	19,830	3,272	0	214,858
46	12	214,858	12,000	10%	22,686	3,743	0	245,801
47	13	245,801	12,000	10%	25,780	4,254	0	279,327
48	14	279,327	12,000	0%	0	4,370	0	286,957
49	15	286,957	12,000	10%	29,896	4,933	0	323,920
50	16	323,920	12,000	10%	33,592	5,543	0	363,970
51	17	363,970	12,000	10%	37,597	6,203	0	407,363
52	18	407,363	12,000	10%	41,936	6,919	0	454,380
53	19	454,380	12,000	10%	46,638	7,695	0	505,323
54	20	505,323	12,000	10%	51,732	8,536	0	560,519
55	21	560,519	12,000	10%	57,252	9,447	0	620,324
56	22	620,324	12,000	-5%	(31,616)	9,011	0	591,698
57	23	591,698	12,000	10%	60,370	9,961	0	654,106
58	24	654,106	12,000	10%	66,611	10,991	0	721,726
59	25	721,726	12,000	10%	73,373	12,106	0	794,992
60	26	794,992	12,000	10%	80,699	13,315	0	874,376
61	27	874,376	12,000	10%	88,638	14,625	0	960,389
62	28	960,389	12,000	10%	97,239	16,044	0	1,053,583
63	29	1,053,583	12,000	10%	106,558	17,582	0	1,154,559
64	30	1,154,559	12,000	10%	116,656	19,248	0	1,263,967
65	31	1,263,967	12,000	10%	127,597	21,053	0	**1,382,510**

$175,344 = $535,271 (FV)

This table adds a column (shaded) to recognize the cost of investment fees and commissions at a rate of 1.5% of Jill's account balance at the end of each year. If we were to total the shaded column, we'd find the gross dollar amount of fees is $175,344 - a huge number to be sure. But she loses the opportunity of having those dollars as part of her wealth building account, so the real impact moves her account balance down another $535,271, or 29.9%.

Now, Jill has about $1.4 million; a full $1,000,000 less than she would have had before we introduced risk and fees.

But we have one more step yet to go. Jill is going to be taxed on her gains. Watch what happens next.

Rigged

Age	Year	Beg Bal	Savings	Growth %	Growth $$	1.5% Fees	25% Taxes	End Bal
35	1	0	12,000	10%	1,200	198	251	12,752
36	2	12,752	12,000	10%	2,475	408	517	26,302
37	3	26,302	12,000	10%	3,830	632	800	40,700
38	4	40,700	12,000	10%	5,270	870	1,100	56,001
39	5	56,001	12,000	5%	3,400	1,071	582	69,747
40	6	69,747	12,000	10%	8,175	1,349	1,706	86,867
41	7	86,867	12,000	10%	9,887	1,631	2,064	105,058
42	8	105,058	12,000	10%	11,706	1,931	2,444	124,389
43	9	124,389	12,000	10%	13,639	2,250	2,847	144,930
44	10	144,930	12,000	10%	15,693	2,589	3,276	166,758
45	11	166,758	12,000	10%	17,876	2,950	3,732	189,953
46	12	189,953	12,000	10%	20,195	3,332	4,216	214,600
47	13	214,600	12,000	10%	22,660	3,739	4,730	240,791
48	14	240,791	12,000	0%	0	3,792	0	248,999
49	15	248,999	12,000	10%	26,100	4,306	5,448	277,344
50	16	277,344	12,000	10%	28,934	4,774	6,040	307,464
51	17	307,464	12,000	10%	31,946	5,271	6,669	339,471
52	18	339,471	12,000	10%	35,147	5,799	7,337	373,482
53	19	373,482	12,000	10%	38,548	6,360	8,047	409,623
54	20	409,623	12,000	10%	42,162	6,957	8,801	448,027
55	21	448,027	12,000	10%	46,003	7,590	9,603	488,836
56	22	488,836	12,000	-5%	(25,042)	7,137	0	468,657
57	23	468,657	12,000	10%	48,066	7,931	10,034	510,758
58	24	510,758	12,000	10%	52,276	8,626	10,913	555,496
59	25	555,496	12,000	10%	56,750	9,364	11,846	603,035
60	26	603,035	12,000	10%	61,504	10,148	12,839	653,552
61	27	653,552	12,000	10%	66,555	10,982	13,893	707,232
62	28	707,232	12,000	10%	71,923	11,867	15,014	764,274
63	29	764,274	12,000	10%	77,627	12,809	16,205	824,888
64	30	824,888	12,000	10%	83,689	13,809	17,470	889,298
65	31	889,298	12,000	10%	90,130	14,871	18,815	**957,742**

Now we've just added a column to calculate the impact of taxes, using an assumed rate of 25% on just the gain each year, bringing our total account crashing down to $957,742.

Jill would have built an account worth $2,401,653 without the big three wealth eroders. With them she is left with $957,000.

- ***Jill put up all the money.***
- ***Jill took all the risk.***
- ***Jill ends up with 40%.***

The <u>market</u>, the <u>broker</u>, and the <u>tax man</u> rob her of 60%

Does that seem possible? Are the deductions I introduced aggressive - or conservative? Could it be worse for Jill - much worse? Does it seem right? Is it what you signed up for when you started your quest for wealth? Is this a picture of YOUR account - with a different name on top and slightly different numbers?

Now can you see why I'm so passionate about exposing losses in the three forms we've identified here?

Let me ask you one last question while we're on this subject. Sometimes those kinds of big numbers seem a bit abstract - hard to put into context. How much different is a $950,000 retirement, than a $2.4 million retirement? If we go by the mainstream rule of thumb, we would take about 4% out of our account each year in retirement income with pretty good assurance we wouldn't run out of money before we run out of days. So,

$2,400,000 X 4% = **$96,000** of annual income

vs.

$957,000 X 4% = **$38,280** of annual income

Is that important to you? If so, then ***<u>you must think defense before you think offense</u>***. You must eliminate the three-headed monster. Fortunately, you've come to the right place - because you can.

Rigged

Chapter 9

The Five Money Needs

You may be at a point where you're ready to throw your hands up and look for a cave you can crawl into. Do not despair. If I didn't have answers, I wouldn't have written the book. We now have a crystal clear idea of what we *don't* want. If there is a way, we want to eliminate the risk of losses, taxes, and high investing fees and commissions.

But it's not enough just to know what we don't want - we need to know what we *do* want?

The starting point for me is what I call the Five Money Needs. These are things we all aspire for our money - and they're things that if achieved, would almost certainly guarantee success at the wealth building game. Let's look at them:

1. **Safety**. We want our money to be safe - we don't want to lose money - ever. There are two kinds of risk that our money faces - one is what we put our money *in* - the other is whom we put our money *with*. We don't want to put it into securities, investments, instruments, or markets that can go down in value. Nor do we want to put it with custodians, advisors, brokerages, or companies that don't have a long, proven track record of trustworthiness and fidelity.

2. **Growth**. We always want to have more money tomorrow - than we have today - always. That eliminates most of the investments you may presently own. It eliminates stocks, bonds, mutual funds, real estate, commodities, precious metals, collectables, options, and most other investments. In fact, it may seem that it eliminates everything that gives us a decent chance at a reasonable retirement. It does not - but we're not there yet. The point is that uninterrupted growth means compounding - and Albert Einstein called compounding the Ninth Wonder of the World for a reason.

3. **Income**. There comes a time in life, when we no longer want to work for an income (or at least work as hard for an income). Instead, we want our money to do the work of providing us an

income. After all - that's what all this hard work and sacrifice has been about. When we rely on our money for an income - we need it to be there - reliably and forever - meaning we don't want it to run out. Rather, we want an inexhaustible income stream we cannot outlive.

4. **Liquidity**. We want to be able to get at our money when we want - particularly in the event of an emergency or an opportunity - and we want to be able to do so without penalty. If we're homeowners, we've already made a decision to store an enormous amount of our wealth in an asset that can not only go down in value, but that is highly illiquid and generates precisely zero return on investment. To then put our liquid cash into illiquid investments and accounts adds more liquidity risk - one of the most devastating and underappreciated financial risks going - which makes no sense at all.

5. **Tax-Efficiency**. Whether we've chosen to accumulate wealth in a qualified plan like an IRA, 401(k) or others; or we've chosen a taxable plan - we face a tax liability - and a tax liability is like having a silent partner in our wealth account. We don't need a silent partner - particularly one who brings nothing to the dance. We want to build wealth tax-efficiently, and the most tax-efficient wealth - is tax-free wealth.

Look back at the list of the Five Money Needs; *Safety, Growth, Income, Liquidity, and Tax-Efficiency*. Notice that three of them are *defensive* in nature; Safety, Liquidity, and Tax-Efficiency. That's completely consistent with the "defense first" theme we've been developing.

The two money needs that are offensive are the needs for Growth and Income - and frankly, income is mostly a function at how well we do growing our money by the time we need it to provide income.

I present the Five Money Needs all over the country at live events. When I do, I always ask my audience a series of questions that I'd like for you to contemplate:

- What is missing from the list?
- What is on the list that is unimportant? Are there money needs that you don't want or need?

- If we could achieve all five money needs, what would our chances of wealth building success be?
- Is your wealth-building portfolio invested in things that meet all five money needs - <u>at the same time</u>?
- If you took the Five Money Needs to your investment advisor and insisted that your portfolio be filled with things that meet them all - what would they say?

The list *is* complete - there is *nothing* missing. The list is important - there is nothing we would give up from the list if we didn't have to. Our chances of success with the Five Money Needs is nearly 100%. And I have yet to find one person who is building wealth in the mainstream world who has one single investment - much less an entire portfolio - that meets all five money needs simultaneously.

How can we agree that these are the things we want - that these are the things that would maximize our chances of success and virtually lock out any chance of failure - yet these are *not* the things we put our money into, nor do we insist that those who help us, put our money into things that meet the Five Money Needs?

From the discussion that's led to this point, I hope the answer is beginning to become clear. Wall Street - Wall Street Advisors - and Wall Street strategies - are designed first for the benefit of...Wall Street. If they can keep us happy with a few crumbs - most of us won't object, and like sheep being led to the slaughter - we'll keep putting more and more money with them, rationalizing them as experts who are acting in our best interest.

Wall Street is well organized, well orchestrated, well coordinated, and well planned. Magazines, newspapers, and personalities reinforce the perception; and the herd mentality it creates gives us a sense of security because "everybody's doing it." You've picked this book up because your gut instinct doesn't reconcile with the Wall Street rationale - and now, we're putting words to some of that discomfort.

There is an answer. There is a different way - but patience is a virtue - so keep reading.

The unarguable fact is - there is nothing - NOTHING - in the Wall Street world that meets all five money need simultaneously. What's worse, we're taught that the more we demand of one money need - the less we'll get of the others.

- **Want more safety?** The greatest safety we can hope for is a bank or a government security - neither of which offer instruments that meet the other Money Needs.
- **Want growth?** We're told we'll have to give up safety. The old Risk-Reward equation, right?
- **Want income - particularly inexhaustible, lifetime income?** We'll have to give up growth.
- **Want more liquidity?** Then don't tie your money up in CDs, bonds, or real estate.
- **Want tax-efficiency?** Good luck.

Trading one money need for another is no good. Unless we have them all - at the same time - we diminish our odds of success. If you never read another page of this book - or even if you do and decide to totally ignore my recommended solution - do this one thing, I implore you. Evaluate your investments and your investing strategies against the Five Money Needs. Tear this page out - take it to your advisor and demand that they fill your portfolio with things that meet all five money needs.

They will not - because they cannot.

There is a way you can - and I will show that way.

Part III -

Wall Street Myths, Lies, and other Deceptions

"There are two kinds of investors, be they large or small; those who don't know where the market is headed, and those who don't know that they don't know. Then again - there is a third type of investor - the investment professional, who indeed knows that he or she doesn't know, but whose livelihood depends upon appearing to know."

William Bernstein, The Intelligent Asset Allocator (New York: McGraw-Hill, 2001)

Rigged

Chapter 10

The Deception of Average Market Returns

Finish this statement: "Over time, nothing you invest in will outperform ____ _____ _____." The answer, of course: ***the stock market***.

When we think of ways of *losing* money with investments, most of us think of the stock market. Interestingly however, when we think of the best way to really *build* wealth, we think of...the stock market.

So most of us would conclude that the stock market is both the best way to lose money - and the best way to build wealth. Most of us would be right - on both counts. The deception is that the statement is incomplete - and like an iceberg that hides most of its destructive power under the surface, so the stock market masks its true risk with well-grounded axioms like, *"nothing will outperform the stock market over time."*

The Compound Annual Growth Rate (CAGR) of the S&P 500 over the last 150 years is about 9% as of this writing. Don't take my word for it - get the actual figure by visiting:

http://www.moneychimp.com/features/market_cagr.htm

I consider this number a WMD - a Weapon of Mass Destruction - of wealth, that is. I say that because the mainstream financial services industry uses it to justify all sorts of assertions - many of which you may have heard from time to time.

- They'll tell you that you have to have at least some stock market exposure or you'll never get to the finish line you dream of.
- They tell you their goal is to out-perform the market.
- When they do - they often use the occasion to justify "locking-in" some profits by selling positions that are up.
- When they're wrong - they use the occasion to sell some positions and "adjust" the investment strategy by buying others (they don't mention that in doing so, you're "locking in" losses).

- When you tell them you're a more conservative investor, they use the occasion to suggest mutual funds as a way of mitigating risk.

Notice two things. They NEVER tell you risk can be completely avoided. In fact, their basket of investment choices contains only a scant few options that could be considered no-risk; certificates of deposit, and money market accounts. But advisors don't make much money on these - and by design - neither do you.

And that leads to the second observation. Changes of direction - adjustments - capturing gains - cutting losses - all these trigger transactions; and transactions are the lifeblood of the mainstreamers - because transactions mean more fees and commissions.

Think of it this way. If there was an investment that grew at 9% per year and never moved backward; a great proportion of investors - perhaps even you - would take that option, dump all you could into that investment, and sit back for 30 years at which time your 7-figure account would be ripe for a lavish retirement.

When the markets tank - as they do every few years, you'd quietly smile to yourself while your friends and neighbors are losing sleep, avoiding the mailbox, and experiencing panic attacks as they watch their account balances tumble.

But if you were able to get consistent 9% returns, what would happen to your poor investment advisor? How would he or she make a living? No transactions - no account churn - no gamesmanship of moving from one broker to another - or from one investment house to another? Take it all away, and we've gutted an entire industry.

Starting to see a different picture emerge here?

But we're just getting started at the unmasking of the deception of market returns.

Even if you accept my 9% number, or another number you're more comfortable with - they're all wrong - and they're wrong because nobody - <u>NOBODY EVER get's the full "market" return</u>. Let me give you a few reasons why.

1. <u>We never own the whole market</u> - The simple fact is, we rarely see the Microsoft's coming; and we rarely avoid the Enrons until it's too late. Few brokers or advisors have the foresight to catch Microsoft at the point where the janitor got in. So by the time a Microsoft is on their radar screen, much of the run-up has already happened. You may still do well - but you won't capture the whole gain. Likewise, by the time companies like Enron look like a real problem, most of us will already have been on the down elevator for quite a while; and a few of us will ride it all the way to the floor. Even if we're smart enough to get out just after the downturn starts, we've locked in a loss and are sitting on the sideline in cash - and therefore don't own the whole market.

2. <u>The Market is tax-inefficient</u> – Whether we take my 9% number, or the one you're more comfortable with; both are subject to taxes, and the simple fact is that 100% of our market gains are taxed as realized. Best case, profits are taxed as long-term capital gains – the lowest of the tax treatments available. But long-term capital gains require holding a position more than one year, which doesn't allow us to be as "nimble" as we may want to be in order to take advantage of opportunities. Additionally, only six states as of this writing (AR, MA, RI, SC, VT, and WI) offer any kind of capital gain treatment when it comes to state income taxes. All the others will tax your gains as ordinary income (the highest rate) no matter how long you've held a position.

3. <u>We Never Capture All Dividends</u> - That 9% figure assumes we capture and reinvest 100% of all dividends. When we're in and out of the market, it is an impossibility of timing to capture and re-invest dividends. While it's true that many stocks don't issue dividends, many do. In fact, the safer investments tend to be the ones that have higher dividends with higher frequency. They also tend to have lower growth in share value - some of which is made up by dividends. And by the way - dividends are taxed at higher ordinary income tax rates.

1. <u>We don't "capture" full market gains</u> – Not only do we not "own" the full market, we wouldn't capture its full gain even if we did. To lock in a gain (or a loss for that matter), we have to

sell a position, whether it's a stock, a bond, or a mutual fund. The simple fact is that we don't know what the high or low point is *until it's in the rearview mirror*.

When we sell a stock that is up, we don't know if it's going to move higher or lower from our exit point. Similarly, we sometimes sell a stock that's down, but we don't know where it's going after our exit point. Therefore, we never capture all the market's gains, nor absorb all the market's losses. Three issues impact what portion of the market's movement we actually capture:

a. **Emotion** – As much as we'd like to believe we act rationally, the fact is, we act emotionally. Where is Warren Buffet when markets "correct" (crash)? He's in cash - there to snap up the bargains because the rest of us are in panic mode, selling at a loss, driving stock prices down; thereby creating the very bargain-priced inventory he buys. In other words, he's not selling on the downswing, he's buying. We're selling.

That means that when the market is up, he's sitting on cash so that he can act on the correction. Where are we when the market is up? Fully invested, running to the mailbox to see how much we made last month.

Investors like Buffet are opportunists; happy to buy when we're selling, and sell when we're buying. Buffett makes a lot of money on our greed and fear – enough in fact, that guys like him out-earn us by a wide margin even when only a portion of their available capital is invested at any given point in time. We, on the other hand, believe that to capture the full benefit of the market, our capital must always be 100% employed.

b. **Mechanics** – When we liquidate a position – whether it's a gain or a loss – we're in cash and on the sideline until a better use for our investment capital comes along. When we're in cash, we're not participating in the market so it's impossible for us to achieve the overall market return.

c. **Re-Entry** - Best-case scenario, we've sold a position at a huge gain. Now we're in cash. When do individual stocks or mutual funds tend to permit us huge gains? When the overall market is up of course. Now what? We're in cash - and the market is up. When do we get back in? At the top? Or - do we wait for the market to come back down so we can re-enter on a low ebb? Where is the bottom of that low ebb? How do we objectively define a good re-entry point? Is it a "finger-in-the-wind" instinct? We may think we know where that bottom is - but we never really know for sure. And even if we did, would we have the guts to shove our chips back onto the table when the market sinks to our arbitrary re-entry point? Re-entry is an imperfect science - and another reason we don't experience the full market gain.

d. **Opportunity** – Without detailing all the commissions, fees, expenses, loads, sales charges, bid and ask spreads, and the numerous other ways the industry makes its money, the fact is, their advice is anything but free. Whatever you believe that "price" might be, it erodes the gains the market might provide – and it does so whether you're a winner, or a loser.

So let's wrap up the "Deception of Market Returns" this way. If we start from the 150 year historical return of the S&P 500 - 9% - then make a deduction for each of the myths we've detailed - where do you end up?

	My Number	Your Number
Historical, Long-term market performance	9.0%	
Deduct: *We never own the whole market*	-0.5%	
Deduct: *We never capture full gains/losses*	-0.5%	
Deduct: *Cost of Fees and Commissions*	-2.0%	
Net Gain Before Income Taxes	=6.0%	
Deduct: *Income Taxes (30% of Gain)*	-1.8%	
Equals net, after-tax return	=4.2%	

If your starting number was lower than mine, you might find yourself in a state of depression right now. Take heart - this book has a happy ending.

If your starting number is higher than mine - and even if your "deducts" are lower than mine, if you're honest with yourself, you'll be hard-pressed to come up with a bottom line number that's much more than 5-6%. If my numbers are 50% too pessimistic, it only boosts the expected return up to 6.3%.

You'll soon discover that there are better, less stressful, more predictable ways to earn more than 4.2% net - in fact, more than 6.3% net - in fact, up to "double-digits" - net, in some cases - because you can get there without risk, without taxes, and without fees.

Chapter 11

The Lie of Risk/Reward

Everybody knows that risk and return are inverse to one another, right? The more risk we're willing to take, the greater the return we can expect - and vice versa. Buy a CD and our money is safe - but we're stuck with a miniscule bit of interest. Buy a big growth stock - and we could double or triple our money - or we could end up with nothing. That's just the way the game works, right? Not so fast grasshopper!

Remember our old friend Warren Buffett? He says rule number one is **"Lose No Money**." I'm pretty sure owners of Buffet's company - Berkshire Hathaway - don't accept CD-like returns on their money. And I'm pretty sure Buffet doesn't deliver CD-like returns. In fact, check out this summary of an in-depth 2005 study regarding Buffet and the share price performance of Berkshire Hathaway:

> Gerald Martin and John Puthenpurackal rigorously examine various possible explanations for Berkshire Hathaway's superior investment performance. Is it luck? Is it reward-for-risk? Is it outstanding stock-picking skill? Using information on 261 common equity investments from Berkshire Hathaway's SEC filings and market databases for 1980-2003, *they conclude that:*
>
> - The mean (median) annualized returns for the stock investments in Berkshire's portfolio from 1980 to 2003 are 39.38% (19.92%).
> - While beating the market in 20 out of 24 years from 1980-2003 is possibly due to randomness at a 5% significance level, the magnitude by which Berkshire beats the market (an average of 12.24% annually) makes "luck" an unlikely explanation.
> - High levels of risk do not explain Berkshire's high returns.
> - Most likely, Warren Buffett is an investor with superior stock-picking skill that allows him to identify undervalued securities and thus obtain risk-adjusted positive abnormal returns.
> - Stock price reactions suggest that the stock market views Berkshire's purchases as positive signals. An investor who mimicked Berkshire Hathaway's portfolio <u>after</u> public disclosure of such could have achieved positive abnormal annual returns of 7%-10%.

How do we explain the third bullet point that *"High levels of risk do not explain Berkshire's high returns?"* Could it really be true that Buffett never makes a losing bet on a stock or a business acquisition? Isn't "Lose No Money" just a cliché with a point? Surely he can't possibly mean - literally - **Lose No Money**?

I put that question to a friend of mine who is a financial advisor to the super-wealthy. In fact, to be a client of his - you have to have a minimum of $10 million of investable assets. He said that for his super-wealthy clients, "lose no money" is completely realistic, and the story he told gives us insight on how the super-wealthy - and people like Warren Buffet - are able to consistently beat the market without taking on anywhere near the level of risk that most investors like you and I take on every day.

Let's say my friend has a client named Thurston Howell, III (dating myself, aren't I). Mr. Howell asks my friend to manage $10 million of his money. He insists that my friend grow his money - the "lose no money" way - the Warren Buffett way.

To deliver the goods, my friend purchases a portfolio of bonds guaranteed to be worth $10 million in exactly one year. He pays $9.6 million for that portfolio of bonds.

After he deployed $9.6 million of Mr. Howell's money into the bond portfolio, my friend puts the remaining $400,000 into Amalgamated Industries stock because he thinks Amalgamated has a very good chance of growing its share price significantly over the next year (in reality, he puts it into Amalgamated call options to further leverage the position - but let's not confuse matters).

- Now if Amalgamated tanks, goes out of business, and the $400,000 of stock goes to zero, where does Mr. Howell stand? He still has exactly $10 million - the guaranteed maturity value of his bond portfolio. He has "lost no money."

- If Amalgamated stays stuck in neutral - and the share price doesn't move - the $400,000 of Amalgamated stock is worth exactly the same $400,000 at the end of the year. Then where is Mr. Howell? Well, he has $10,000,000 from his bonds, plus $400,000 of Amalgamated stock, for a tidy profit of $400,000 for the year. Not so good on a percentage basis - 4% - but hey, with $400,000 he buys a new Mercedes and takes Lovey on a month-long Mediterranean cruise - and still has $200,000 to live on for the rest of the year. Not too shabby.

- But what if my friend was right - and Amalgamated's share price rose 30% so that Mr. Howell's $400,000 position is now worth $520,000. Now Mr. Howell adds a nice diamond for Lovey on the cruise, buys a country club membership at Augusta National, and lives the "even-better" life.

My friend has just accomplished for Mr. Howell - a "lose no money" way of building wealth - *even if he lost $400,000 on Amalgamated*. So it turns out, Buffet's rule (and by extension, mine) is totally realistic and is exercised every day by those who are truly in the know.

Meanwhile, back on planet earth - here we are. What do we tend to do that's different than Mr. Howell?

Well let's say our own advisor is just as smart as my friend. He or she advises us to buy Amalgamated Industries, "it's gonna fly." We might not have $10,000,000 to play with - but perhaps we have $10,000 to invest. So let's try it the Buffet way. We buy a $10,000 bond portfolio just like Mr. Howell - at a 4% discount - for $9,600. That leaves us with $400 to plunk down on some Amalgamated Industries stock.

Amalgamated does fly, and we're gleeful about the 30% increase in the share price. Our $400 position is now worth $520 - but for some reason, we're not quite as excited because let's face it - our $120 gain won't even get our "Lovey" a half-day at the local strip center day spa.

The point is obvious, we *can't* play the game the way Buffett does - or the way my friend is able to manage his high net worth clients' money. It takes a lot of capital to do it that way. And most of us just don't have the investing inertia to play along at home.

So what do we do instead? We take that tip from our advisor, and put our entire $10,000 *directly* into Amalgamated Industries. Our position is what the insiders call "naked" - we're totally exposed if Amalgamated peters out. If it does, we're out $10,000 - or a good chunk of it. In other words, we've taken the most sage of all advice - given to us freely from the world's greatest investor - and promptly said thanks but no thanks - and thrown it out the window.

Admit it. These are the kinds of investing bets we tend to make every day. They're the kinds of recommendations we get from our most trusted advisors on a regular basis. And it's only because our thinking is constrained by the products and strategies offered up by mainstreamers, that we keep doing it the same dumb way day after day - year after year.

What if there was another way? What if we could do it the "lose no money" way without needing $10,000,000 to do so? In fact, what if we could invest the "lose no money" way with as little as $100/month - or even move what we've already saved into a "lose no money" strategy? Would you want to know more? Aah - the plot thickens!

Chapter 12

The Diversification Deception

If you're getting a bit cynical - like I am - you're starting to realize that mainstreamers don't want risk-free, because they need the "churn" to drive their fee and commission gravy train. But too much risk can get them fired (and you - broke), so they've got to come up with some middle ground that looks like risk-management without compromising account churn.

So they've come up with cute little strategies to create the illusion of safety, which really only nibble around the edges rather than providing true safety. Here are just a couple you may have heard about from the mainstreamers:

> **Diversification** - the practice of buying a variety of instruments with different risk profiles so that if one goes down, the others can hold the ship afloat.

> **Dollar Cost Averaging** - the practice of buying a little bit of a position at a time regardless of the share price. Buy 100 shares at $14, another 100 shares a month later at $12, another 100 shares the following month at $18 - and so on. Theory being that the "blended" or "weighted" cost of the shares is not subject to a temporary anomaly that may have moved the share price up or down when you purchased it.

Sometimes, an advisor will recommend we put both of these risk-management strategies together at the same time - by recommending mutual funds.

Mutual funds are collections of investment instruments assembled by supposedly really smart people (smarter than your local investment advisor). They're often recommended by your local investment advisor who - supposedly - is smart enough to be able to distinguish the really smart mutual fund managers from the ordinarily smart ones.

In fact, some large brokerage firms offer their own proprietary, in-house mutual funds because they think they've hired a bunch of stock pickers who are smarter than your investment advisor - whom they've also hired - and who are smarter than the other mutual fund managers out there who aren't smart enough to be working directly for them.

Confused yet?

If this whole ruse seems as ludicrous to you as it does to me - let's call mutual funds what they are: a way where one advisor (yours) can recommend another advisor (the mutual fund manager), in exchange for a fee that **you** pay in the name of "diversifying your risk."

While mutual funds might be the mainstreamer's best answer to risk-management, let's circle back to where we started this discussion - talking about the deception of diversification. The bottom line is that only when we accept the proposition that risk is a necessary part of wealth building do we have to figure out a way to manage it - whether with mutual funds, dollar-cost-averaging, or some other tactic.

The truth is, diversification serves *them* more than it serves *us*. Does it serve us at all? Yes - but only if we're investing in risk-oriented instruments. If we're not investing in risk-oriented instruments, diversification is completely unnecessary.

Think back to the questions we asked at the end of our chapter on *Lose No Money*. If we could put our money into an instrument that generated a reasonable return year in and year out - an instrument that could never go down no matter what happens in the broader market, what value would diversification add in our quest for wealth? None. We'd simply fund the investment - add money as aggressively as we could - and let it grow and compound. We'd never need to switch investments, turn our accounts over, or diversify our risk - because we wouldn't have any.

That's the goal. So as diversification goes - it's great stuff if we restrict our investing options to risk-oriented holdings - but a complete waste of time, money, and thought energy if we don't.

I'll make this short. Risk is best avoided altogether, not "managed."

Chapter 13

More Mutual Fund Mayhem

As we discussed earlier, mutual funds purport to give their owners access to the best and brightest minds that evaluate and pick the best stocks and other fund holdings – gurus who would otherwise be completely inaccessible to the common man. Minds that are far superior to yours - and even to your advisor. They claim to have staffs of green-eye-shaded forensic investigators who can see into the future, and provide the kind of diversity that will reduce your downside risk.

The resulting industry has hundreds and hundreds of mutual funds. They're typically categorized by their objectives (growth vs. income vs. bonds, etc.). Ninety percent of the funds in any given category produce returns that are within a few percentage points of one another over a 10-year period.

What does this tell us? It tells us that one mutual fund's gurus really aren't much better or worse than the other mutual fund's gurus. Why? Because they're all picking from the same basket of underlying investments.

A sort of cottage industry has grown up which uses software to compare the overlap in holdings among mutual funds. At www.overlap.com for example, for a small fee, you can see exactly how many identical stocks, industry groupings, and risk profiles are held commonly by various mutual funds. You'll be surprised to learn that even funds with different overall objectives can have a great deal of overlap in their holdings. Kind of blows the whole diversification thing - doesn't it?

And when we consider those who invest through a company-sponsored 401(k) or similar qualified plan, often the *only* investment choices are mutual funds. The selection gives the impression of diversification; but the reality is often quite different.

Unfortunately, we're not done with our friends in the mutual fund industry. Growth in mutual funds are never taxed as capital gains, even when held more than one year. Rather, their gains are calculated annually and distributed as dividends - which are taxed as ordinary income - the highest rate. This makes mutual funds the least tax-efficient way to invest in the stock market.

Finally, let's talk fees. All mutual funds involve fees - and their fee layer is typically *in addition to* whatever your local broker may be charging for their services, which can be substantial on its own. Mutual funds that use brokers to sell their shares typically compensate the brokers by imposing a "sales load" which is paid to the selling brokers. In this respect, a sales load is like a commission investors pay when they purchase any type of security from a broker.

Fortunately, the highest sales load allowable by law is a mere 8.5%. Sales loads can come in the form of front-end or back-end charges. If a fund charges a front-end fee of 5%, then when we invest $10,000 in that fund, our beginning account balance is just $9,500. We're 5% in the hole before the first trading day opens - which means we have to earn 5.25% just to get back to our starting point ($9,500 + 5.25% = $10,000).

And remember what we said way back in Chapter 5 about the impact of a 5% loss? We said that it will result in 20.1% less money at the end of the day - and that it can never be recaptured. In the case of these kinds of funds, the minute you purchase a share, you're 20.1% behind the 8-ball - and you'll never make it up - ever.

Other funds charge a back-end fee. Back-end charges are assessed against the balance in your account when you sell the fund. If the mutual fund has done what it said it would do - grow your money - they get a greater commission down the road in dollar terms because of the higher ending balance. Remember what we said about taxes in Chapter 6 - how we're taking a silent partner along with us for the duration of the ride in the form of the tax-man? Well, a mutual fund with back-end fees is just like having a second silent partner who can't wait for you to cash out - and collect their dues. If it's starting to seem like a whole lot of people get paid before you do - you're absolutely right.

Some funds call themselves "no-load" funds. As the name implies, this means that the fund does not charge any type of sales load. But there are a number of fees and costs associated with mutual funds that don't fall in the "sales load" category. It doesn't make them cheaper - it just means the particular fund manager has decided to dispense with the aggravation of being characterized as a "load" fund - and has instead, disguised what would otherwise be a load fee under some other label.

For example, a no-load fund is permitted to charge purchase fees, redemption fees, exchange fees, and account fees, none of which is considered to be a "sales load."

In addition, industry rules allow a fund to deduct its annual operating expenses from our money, and still call itself "no-load." Here is a summary of the various kinds of fees charged by mutual funds and what they're for:

Redemption Fee - A redemption fee is sometimes charged when fund shares are sold. Although a redemption fee is deducted from redemption proceeds just like a deferred sales load, it is not considered to be a sales load. Go figure. Unlike a sales load, which is used to pay brokers, a redemption fee is typically used to defray fund costs associated with a shareholder's redemption and is paid directly to the fund, not to a broker. The SEC limits redemption fees to 2%.

Exchange Fee - An exchange fee is a fee that some funds impose when we exchange (transfer) our money from one fund to another fund within the same fund group or family.

Account Fee - An account fee is a fee that some funds separately impose on investors in connection with the maintenance of their accounts. Sometimes we think if we invest directly with the mutual fund rather than through a broker or investment advisor, we're escaping account fees and loads. Unfortunately, that's often not the case.

Purchase Fee - A purchase fee is sometimes charged when we put money into a mutual fund. I know - sounds like the sales loads we talked about earlier. But a purchase fee differs from, and is not considered to be, a front-end sales load because a purchase fee is paid to the fund (not to a broker) and is typically imposed to defray some of the fund's costs associated with the purchase.

Management Fees - Management fees are paid out of fund assets (our money) to the fund's investment advisor for managing the fund's investment portfolio, and administrative fees payable to the investment advisor that are not included in the "Other Expenses" category (discussed below). Is it all starting to sound very confusing - not to mention expensive? By the way, the investment advisor in this case is the guy/gal picking investments for the fund. So we get to pay them for their advice after we've paid our own financial advisor for picking the fund. Cozy isn't it?

Distribution [and/or Service] (12b-1) Fees - These are fees paid out of fund assets to cover distribution expenses and sometimes shareholder service expenses. "12b-1 fees" get their name from the SEC rule that authorizes a fund to pay them. Distribution fees are paid out of fund assets only if the fund has adopted a plan (12b-1 plan) authorizing their payment, and include fees paid for marketing and selling fund shares, such as compensating brokers and others who sell fund shares, and paying for advertising, the printing and mailing of prospectuses to new investors, and the printing and mailing of sales literature. 12b-1 fees that are used to pay marketing and distribution expenses (as opposed to shareholder service expenses) cannot exceed 0.75 percent of a fund's average net assets per year.

Some 12b-1 plans also authorize and include "shareholder service fees," which are fees paid to persons to respond to investor inquiries and provide investors with information about their investments. A fund may pay shareholder service fees without adopting a 12b-1 plan. If shareholder service fees are part of a fund's 12b-1 plan, these fees will be included in this category of the fee table. If shareholder service fees are paid outside a 12b-1 plan, then they will be included in the "Other expenses" category, discussed below. FINRA imposes an annual .25% cap on shareholder service fees (regardless of whether these fees are authorized as part of a 12b-1 plan). Got it?

Other Expenses - Are expenses not included in the categories "Management Fees" or "Distribution [and/or Service] (12b-1) Fees." Examples include: shareholder service expenses that are not included in the "Distribution [and/or Service] (12b-1) Fees" category; custodial expenses; legal expenses; accounting expenses; transfer agent expenses; and other administrative expenses.

<u>Total Annual Fund Operating Expenses</u> - This line of the fee table is the total of a fund's annual fund operating expenses, expressed as a percentage of the fund's average net assets.

But there's more bad news to come. Mutual funds promote themselves on the basis of what they call their "average annual return." But buried in this incestuous love triangle between you - your advisor, and those mutual funds - is a lie that no one has ever shared with you - a lie that exposes the whole rotten scheme - a scheme that is better demonstrated than explained. To do that, let's go back to our old friend the story problem.

> Question: If Sam puts $1,000 into an investment and earns a 20% average annual return for two years, how much will Sam have two years out?

> > A. $1,440

> > B. $1,280

> > C. $800

> > D. $0.00

> > E. All the Above

The correct answer? E. - All the above.

Wait a minute - this is math. Math can have only one correct answer - so what gives?

It may be math, but it's math according to the mainstream Wall Street world (including mutual funds and those who promote and support them). Here's what I mean.

A. Sam's $1,000 grows by 20% the first year - to $1,200. It grows by another 20% the second year - to $1,440. So answer "A" is correct - and the way most of us would solve the math problem - and the way Wall Street wants us to solve the math problem (+20% + 20% = 40% / 2 years = 20% Average Annual Return).

B. Sam put his $1,000 into an investment that gains 60% the first year - to $1,600, but the next year, he loses 20% of his $1,600, leaving him with $1,280 - answer "B." His average return is still 20% (+60% - 20% = 40% / 2 years = 20% Average Annual Return).

C. Sam put his $1,000 into an investment that doubles the first year - to $2,000, but then suffers a 60% loss the next - leaving him with $800 - answer "C." His average return is still 20% (+100% - 60% = 40% / 2 years = 20% Average Annual Return).

D. Sam put his $1,000 into an investment that grows by 140% the first year - to $1,400; then the investment goes worthless the second year - and Sam is left with zero. According to the Wall Streeters once again, Sam has an average return of 20% (+140% - 100% = 40% / 2 years = 20%).

While Sam's results may seem extreme, the point is 100% valid - this is exactly how Wall Street calculates and quotes "Average Annual Returns." They do it for broad markets, individual stocks, stock indices, and yes - mutual funds. Let's see how this plays out in a more realistic manner. If a mutual fund goes down by 10% one year, then up by 20% the next, what is the average return? Show your work!

Okay we have:	-10
Followed by:	+20
	=10 divided by 2 years = 5% Average Annual Growth

Therefore, it might be reasonable to expect that had we put $1,000 into that fund two years ago, it would now be worth $1,102.50. Why? Because the average two-year return was 5%. Five percent compounded for two years would grow our $1,000 to $1,102.50. Pretty straightforward. But here's what really happens:

Beginning Balance:	$1,000
Year 1 (10% loss)	$ 900
Year 2 (20% gain)	$1,080
Two Year Gain:	$80 divided by 2 years = 4% Compound Annual Growth Rate

Which is it? The 5% they publish in all their material - or is it the 4% that would have been the actual result on the real money we sunk into that fund over that exact period of time?

The answer is 4%. But not according to the industry publications you could find that reference that mutual fund. They would report their average return as 5% - as would their own circulars and brochures - to "independent" publications, and your local advisor at Big Firm Brokerage.

Wait a minute - Houston - we have a problem. The problem is that the "Average Annual Return" is absolutely, completely, totally, utterly, positively ... meaningless.

The difference between 4% and 5% may not sound like a big deal - but that's a 20% difference in favor of the mutual fund company. How can that be? How can the mainstreamers get away with that?

Because their math is *not incorrect - it is incomplete*. It doesn't tell the whole story. And why would they do that? Because it's easier to get you off your wallet for a 5% return than it is for a 4% return.

Think it's just coincidence - they couldn't possibly be that sinister? Think again. Let's do the math their way, but **without any loss years**. Let's say their return in one year was 12%, and the next it was 18%. What would they publish then? Show your work.

Year One: +12

Year Two: +18

=30, divided by two years = 15% average return.

That mutual fund - and all their mainstream co-conspirators, would publish their average return as 15% for that two-year period.

But what would happen - as we did before - when we apply the average annual return to real money?

Beginning Balance:	$1,000
Year 1 (12% gain)	$1,120
Year 2 (18% gain)	$1, 322
Two Year Gain:	$ 322 divided by 2 years = 16.1%/yr!

Wait a minute - that's just the opposite of before. They'd publish an average return of 15% but real compound annual growth rate on our money would have been 16.1%? Why wouldn't they want to publish the larger number?

Here's the answer to the riddle.

Whenever a loss is introduced into the math, the "Average Annual Return" will always be higher than the result when applied to real money. The mutual fund industry has to be consistent - they have to choose one way to do the math - or the other - and once they make that decision, they have to stick with it.

The truth is *they KNOW there will be losses from time to time*, and because there are always - always loss years, they'd rather use the mathematical "Average Annual Return" because it will always give them the better - more saleable figure. If they knew there'd never be a loss - they'd do just the opposite, and publish the Compound Annual Growth Rate (CAGR) instead.

Remember back in Chapter 9 when I introduced you to the website:

> http://www.moneychimp.com/features/market_cagr.htm

In math-speak, they make this very point in the following way:

> A problem with talking about average investment returns is that there is real ambiguity about what people mean by "average". For example, if you had an investment that went up 100% one year and then came down 50% the next, you certainly wouldn't say that you had an average return of 25% = (100% - 50%)/2, because your principal is back where it started: your real annualized gain is zero.
>
> In this example, the 25% is the simple average, or "arithmetic mean". The zero percent that you really got is the "geometric mean", also called the "annualized return", or the "CAGR" for Compound Annual Growth Rate.
>
> Volatile investments are frequently stated in terms of the simple average, rather than the CAGR that you actually get. (Bad news: the CAGR is smaller.)
>
> This calculator lets you find the annualized growth rate of the S&P 500 over the date range you specify; <u>you'll find that the CAGR is usually about a percent or two less than the simple average.</u>

Do you see what I underlined in that last sentence? Do you think 2% would make a difference in your investing portfolio? It makes a huge difference! Did you also pick up that this little mathematical trick isn't restricted just to mutual funds - but rather is commonly used by the entire financial industry when reporting average returns? That means stock market returns - average returns of individual stocks, industry groupings, everything! This ought to make your blood boil. If you think

I've been a little close to the edge of the conspiracy spectrum up till now, you may be starting to see why.

And just when you thought we were done trashing mutual funds - there's more.

Let's say we put $10,000 into a typical mutual fund whose underlying investment portfolio grows by 10%. Before fees - our $10,000 would be worth $11,000 in just a year.

But the mutual fund company has a back-end load of 5%, and during that year, assessed all owners of the fund an expense charge of 1.5%. So if we were to sell our position and lock in our profits, the total fees would be $715 ($11,000 X 5% = $550, plus $11,000 X 1.5% = $165. Those fees consume 71.5% of the $1,000 of economic gain we would have been entitled to. We get a check for $10,285 instead of $11,000 - for a net gain of 2.85% - *before taxes*.

Even more perplexing, the percentage of the gain consumed by the fees goes UP if the growth is less - and goes DOWN if the growth is greater.

Fees are a little like the house odds in Vegas. They seem small. They may still allow us a good chance of winning any given hand - but their cumulative effect can be devastating. Mutual funds may be a good way for those without a large enough account balance to efficiently diversify their investments, but since we now know that the whole concept of diversification is a ruse - my advice is RUN.

One final note. Take a look at the following paragraph directly from the Federal Government's website:

> "As you might expect, fees and expenses vary from fund to fund. A fund with high costs must perform better than a low-cost fund to generate the same returns for you. Even small differences in fees can translate into large differences in returns over time. For example, if you invested $10,000 in a fund that produced a 10% annual return before expenses and had annual operating expenses of 1.5%, then after 20 years you would have roughly $49,725. But if the fund had expenses of only 0.5%, then you would end up with $60,858."

What's the difference between $49,725 and $60,858? 22.4%. Remember how our one-time 5% investment loss resulted in 20.1% less money at the end - money that could never be recovered? Here we have even more devastating math, because when that little, tiny 1%

difference in fees repeats itself every year for 20 years, it's 22.4% less money. And 20 years is more than half of a typical investing lifetime.

Chapter 14

The Myth of Recoveries

When the market does "correct" (broker speak for "crash"), it can take a long time to get back into winning territory. And that time may catch us at an inconvenient stage of life. If we've just retired, or are about to retire, and the market takes one of its 20% dives - or worse - it can be a real problem. We might have to make significant and even permanent adjustments in our lifestyle. We might have to defer our retirement for a few years. We might have to get really good at saying, "Welcome to Wal-Mart."

If we're 28 on the other hand, market corrections may not seem like such a big deal. But they are, and they bear a closer examination. So let's take a look at market recoveries.

Consider the great stock market crash of 1929. The market did not achieve its pre-1929 level until 1954 – a full 25 years later. So if, in 1929, you were about to retire, those plans were put on hold - probably for the rest of your life. If you were just starting your investing life in 1929 however - by 1954, you would have made a killing.

Most consider 1929 to 1954 an historic anomaly - something that's not relevant to a discussion about recoveries in our new, modern age. There are new rules, "circuit breakers," and other safeguards that would save us from another 1929 - right?

Well even with those, the reality is that the average bear market (more than a 20% correction) requires nearly 15 years to get back into positive territory. Besides - all the circuit breakers, technology and other rules haven't saved the Japanese.

The Nikkei 225 – Japan's equivalent of the S&P 500, reached its peak of just short of 40,000 points on December 29, 1989. Today, it sits well under 10,000 - and has languished there for the last several years (with the odd spike from time to time). That's more than two decades, and the Nikkei has never even threatened its previous highs in the time since. In fact, the Nikkei 225 closed 1981 at about where it is today - and that's now more than 32 years in the past - _seven years longer_ than the post "Great Depression" US market recovery that took from 1929 to

1954. In fact, the Nikkei isn't even at a quarter of what it must get to in order to claim "recovery."

But that's Japan - it couldn't happen to that degree in the modern day United States right? Well it turns out - we're just emerging from a 13-year long bear market in the US today.

In the closing days of 2009, the Wall Street Journal published an article that calls the decade of the 2000's the worst decade for the stock market in its history. According to WSJ reporter Tom Lauricella:

> *"The U.S. stock market is wrapping up what is likely to be its worst decade ever.*
>
> *In nearly 200 years of recorded stock-market history, no calendar decade has seen such a dismal performance as the 2000s.*
>
> *Investors would have been better off investing in pretty much anything else, from bonds to gold or even just stuffing money under a mattress. Since the end of 1999, stocks traded on the New York Stock Exchange have lost an average of 0.5% a year thanks to the twin bear markets this decade."*

As of this writing, it's more than three years later - and the story is little changed. We saw a decent gain in 2010, but 2011 was dead flat and 2012 was up again. Despite these gains, we remain in a 13-year stretch where the market has given us very little on a net basis.

The point is this. Even if we buy the argument that the stock market performs better than other investments over the long run, "the long run" can be problematic. Most of us have an accumulation phase of 30-40 years (from age 25 to age 65), and most of that is heavily back-end loaded when our income is at its peak. That means our ability to achieve those long-term gains is as much a matter of chance (when our 40-year accumulation window opens and closes), as it is our ability to pick stocks. I call that Chronological Russian Roulette - and that's not a plan at all, because we often don't have time to wait out the correction of a sustained bear market.

Retirees exposed to the market in the 2008 meltdown know this all too well. Panicked investors - perhaps even you or people you know - were burning up the phone lines of their investment advisors desperately seeking advice on what to do. They were told to hang in there - the markets have to come back.

Now just think about that for a moment. What else would you expect an advisor to say? They can't say, "let's buy more on the dip" because they're panicked too. They can't say, "let's sell," because it would mean moving you from a paper loss to an actual loss - which would destroy whatever "value" and credibility those investment advisers clung to.

In 2008, some couldn't take the pressure, and sold anyway (which tells me their advisor didn't do a good job of truly assessing their risk tolerance in the first place - and should never have let them buy those securities). But then again - a broker would probably never get a new client again if they forced their clients to answer the question - *"what will you do or how will you feel if we're ever down 40%?"*

Most of those who stuck it out in 2008 have recovered most of that loss by now, but hundreds of thousands who were retired or have retired since, have had to adjust their lifestyles dramatically and permanently as a result - a tragedy that could have been completely avoided. If the market continues to sputter, many people – people you know – will have to join them, resigning themselves to a lifestyle that they wouldn't have had to consider even a few years ago were it not for their exposure to the market.

As if the timeline of recoveries wasn't bad enough, the "math" of a recovery can be downright depressing. One reason bear markets take so long to recover is math. In 2008, a $100,000 account shrunk to about $60,000 on average. To regain the $100,000 starting point, the market must gain almost 70% ($60,000 X 170% = $102,000).

So let's say your account balance in 2007 was $100,000; and that by the end of 2008, it had plummeted to just $60,000. Then - luck turned your way, and your account had an unprecedented, uninterrupted 10-year run with consistent gains of 12% per year – with no down years or mini-corrections in between, just straight up - like a rocket ship. It's never happened by the way - but this is just hypothetical - so let's dream.

Your account would have clawed its way back to $186,350 - a spectacular recovery to be sure. That's 12 years (2 down years followed by 10 up years) for our original $100,000 to not quite double, representing a compound annual growth rate of 4.7%. What? And that's 4.7% in an unprecedented - ideal scenario.

It's not a great number. And remember, Uncle Sam wants his share of the $86,350 gain, which I haven't even considered in this example.

What's worse - those 12 years consumed about 1/3 of a typical investor's investing lifetime. Do you think 1/3 of your investing lifetime - to get 4.7% - before taxes and investment fees - is a good deal? Do you think that perhaps you could have put your money into something much safer and still earned 4.7% - and held on to the years of life expectancy that the terror of 2008 sucked out of you?

The table below ties this discussion all together. It shows how long it takes our money to crawl back to break-even, given various losses and various recovery rates.

If you Lose...	At 3% growth, you'll recover in..	At 6% growth, you'll recover in..	At 8% growth, you'll recover in..
10%	3.6 Years	1.8 Years	1.3 Years
20%	7.5 Years	3.7 Years	2.9 Years
30%	12.0 Years	6.0 Years	4.6 Years
40%	17.0 Years	8.6 Years	6.6 Years
50%	23.2 Years	11.6 Years	9.0 Years

Now you know why your advisor recommends a "direction shift" when you lose money. They know the recovery time is long and that your patience might not be equal to the task. Better to absorb the loss - and get on to something with a higher likelihood of getting you back above water more quickly, than staying put and waiting for a miracle. And by the way - in making that recommendation, who collects another commission?

Chapter 15

The Account Statement Deception

Ready for the shortest chapter in the book? Here goes - and it's important. Imagine you just picked up the mail and opened it on your way back into the house. "Honey, great news. Our account statement says we were up 6.4% last month!"

Sorry Charlie - you're not up 6.4% - no matter what that piece of paper says.

Let's say our ending balance from the previous month was $100,000 - and our ending balance this month is $106,400 - our 6.4% gain. Here are five reasons why we can't get a check for $106,400:

1. On the day, minute, and second that statement was printed - we may have been up 6.4%, but before the ink even dried, the market had moved, and the statement was wrong. But hey - how much could it have moved in the day or two it was in the mail? Besides, if its moved, that means you could be up, right? Right - but up or down - the statement is wrong.

2. If I sell my holdings and move into spendable cash - my broker wants to eat too - so he or she is going to take a piece of my action - just a small piece - so I'm not too upset about it (although it is a bit aggravating that they get paid regardless of how I come out) - but oh well - those are the rules of the conventional game.

3. Let's say I get lucky and net $106,000 on the sale of those securities after my broker's fees. Uncle Sam says I have a $6,000 taxable gain. Whether I'm taxed at the capital gain rate or the ordinary income rate doesn't really matter - it's a big bite out of my apple that renders my account statement meaningless.

4. Then the state piles on for their share.

5. If my gain is considered ordinary income - that $6,000 gain will be added to whatever other money I made that year - salary,

profit, dividends, my wife's income, etc. - and could drive up the tax rate on all the rest of my income too.

Whatever I end up with once I've paid everybody up and down the mainstream food chain for my great fortune - I now have another problem. Every day I sit on the cash - I'm not growing my wealth.

Chapter 16

The Liquidity Deception

When we talk about risk, most people naturally think about losing money. Few think about their liquidity risk. Liquidity is the measure of how much of our money we can get at - and how quickly we can get at it - when we need it. Liquidity risk is huge, misunderstood, and underestimating it can be devastating.

Several of the most popular investments and investment accounts impose huge liquidity risk on us, and too often, we don't discover the cost of liquidity risk until it's too late and we can't avoid being touched by it.

Qualified Plans impose a liquidity risk because the arrangement we have made with our partner - Uncle Sam - is that we won't access our money until retirement - or to be more specific, until at least age 59-1/2. There are some limited exceptions to this which we'll leave for another time.

We're often lured into the lair of qualified plans because of the seemingly obvious tax advantages they offer. Company-sponsored qualified plans often have a second enticement - matching contributions. But what happens if we have an emergency or an opportunity? Perhaps a child becomes ill and needs expensive care that exceeds our insurance coverage. Or perhaps a child is unexpectedly offered admission to a prestigious - but expensive college.

It's for these very kinds of "life" events that we save and invest in the first place. But when we've saved and invested through qualified plans, we've voluntarily agreed to accept an additional 10% surtax (penalty) for getting at our money prior to retirement.

So when Johnny or Suzy's tuition is going to be $50,000 a year for that prestigious private school with the good education in his/her field of interest - instead of the $12,000 a year for the state college you planned on - you need to get around $150,000 more over the next four years. If you take that out of your 401(k), you need to "gross up" the withdrawal by at least 40% so you have money to pay the tax and penalties that will apply to your withdrawal. That means you'll need to take out $250,000 so that after tax and penalty, you have $150,000 to make those tuition payments.

Where did I come up with 40%? I assumed a tax rate of 30%, plus the 10% penalty. If you're breathing a little sigh of relief because you're not in the 30% tax bracket - think again. When you take $50,000 out of the 401(k), it's added to your regular income for tax purposes - *that year*. So if your normal marginal tax rate was 20% based on your income, it may well be 30% based on your normal income PLUS $50,000.

Chances are, you know somebody who has lost a job. Perhaps their company had a great matching plan for contributions the employee made to the company 401(k) plan. So they saved with a vengeance to take advantage of all that free money from the employer. In fact, they were so committed to being voracious savers, that they didn't save money outside the 401(k) plan.

Now they're out of work - with little in the bank to pay next month's bills. What to do? Take a withdrawal from the 401(k) - and pay the accompanying penalty (in addition to the tax)? Bye-bye matching funds - you just gave them all to Uncle Sam as the price for getting at what a minute ago - you thought was your own money.

Certificate of Deposit owners have known about liquidity risk for a long time. If we buy a longer term CD, we get a higher interest rate than we do with a short-term CD. So why not always buy long-term CD's? Because if we have to get at our money, we have a "substantial penalty for early withdrawal." So we often give up "return" in order to preserve liquidity.

The liquidity risk touches homeowners most directly. Chances are your parents told you that home ownership should be one of your loftiest financial goals. The reasoning is that "rent" goes down the drain and we have nothing to show for it - but when we buy a home, at least we're building "equity." As far as that advice goes, Mom and Dad are right.

The problem is that we focus on the benefits of ownership (the buildup of equity), and ignore the liquidity risk of ownership. What is the liquidity risk of ownership? How much - and how quickly we can get at our money?

Let's say 10 years ago, we bought a $150,000 home, with a 20% down payment, or $30,000. The principal portion of our payments over the 10 years has added another $70,000 of equity - so we now have

$100,000 of equity in our home. Pretty good, right? But how much of our money can we get at - and how quickly can we get at it?

We have two options - sell the house - or take out a home equity loan. Neither is fast, and both mean "paying" to get at our own money. We pay in the form of real estate commissions and closing fees to sell the house - and we pay in the form of application fees, appraisal fees, and loan origination fees with the home equity loan option - and that's before we pay rent (interest) each month on the borrowed money - which we thought was our own money - and now we're right back into the very "rent-goes-down-the-drain" thing we were told to avoid in the first place.

Liquidity is the least understood, and most underestimated of the various forms of financial risk.

Rigged

Chapter 17

The "Bond" Myth

In my live seminars, I'll often ask people to identify what they consider to be risk-free investments. The list is always short, but invariably, someone will propose that bonds are risk-free. It's not hard to see how they arrive at that conclusion. After all, if we buy a $1,000 bond and we're committed to holding it - we know exactly what it will be worth at maturity. Sounds like no risk doesn't it? But like most myths of mainstream origin, a bit more explanation is required before we lock in our final answer about the risk-free nature of bonds. First, let's separate bonds into three common categories:

1. Tax-Free Municipal Bonds,
2. Government-issued bonds (savings bonds and treasuries)
3. Corporate bonds

Governments issue the first two. Since we believe governments to be safe, we consider that our principal investment is safe. That's less true than it once was - just ask Standard & Poors who, in 2011 downgraded the safety of US Government debt obligations (bonds). Or - ask the people of California where three of the state's largest cities have declared bankruptcy, eliminating their bond obligations, and costing investors billions in bond principal.

But let's set that aside for the moment. There are three variables that determine the value of a bond:

- The face, or maturity value;
- the interest rate,
- and the maturity date.

So let's say we buy a typical $1,000 bond with a 4% interest coupon, and a 10-year maturity. Each year - for the next 10 years, we'll get a check for $40 of interest - and at the end of 10 years, we'll "redeem" our bond for exactly its $1,000 face value. It's the in-between - what happens during those 10 years - that is the difference.

When we bought the bond, prevailing interest rates may have been 4%, but what if prevailing interest rates move upward to 5%? We could buy a new bond with a 5% coupon rate, and earn $50 of interest for the same $1,000. Because of this, the "open market" might be willing to buy our bond if we needed to move into cash - but with a 4% coupon rate, they won't pay the same price they will for a brand new 5% bond.

Instead, the market will re-value our bond by dividing its $40 annual interest payment by the new, 5% rate they could get on a new bond, making our bond worth only $800 ($40 annual interest divided by 5% prevailing interest rate = $800) on the open market.

So much for the safety of bonds. If we wanted to - or needed to move back into cash, we would have to sell the bond at the market value of just $800, and we'd lose $200 of our principal. But - you say - you don't intend to sell your bond on the open market, so it truly is risk-free. Hold it to maturity, and you've got your $1,000 back - no loss. True - sort of.

You may have preserved your principal and avoided the market risk, but you've suffered another kind of cost - an opportunity cost - the opportunity of earning 5% on your money rather than 4%. That $10 of annual interest you gave up is worth $100 over 10 years, several hundred over 40 years when compounded (because we know that an opportunity cost can never be recovered).

So whether you sell or hold, there is a risk associated with bonds that is often overlooked. You either pay it in the form of a discounted market value - or you pay it in the form of a lost opportunity cost that can never be recovered.

Could the math work the other way? Could your bond be worth more if interest rates moved down? Absolutely. Applying the same math in an interest rate environment that moved down to 3% would make our 4% bond worth $1,333 on the open market - but the same logic applies. We'd have to buy a new bond at the lower interest rate if we still wanted the safety of bonds - then we'd be exposed if interest rates climbed again.

Bonds do offer safety when purchased in maturities that make sense for a given situation - they're just not risk-free in the way the mainstreamers would have you believe.

Chapter 18

The Lie of Home Ownership

Myth: *"The equity in my home is a good investment since real estate values always go up over time."*

Another two-part myth. Let's deal with the second part, first (confusing isn't it) - the part that says real estate values always go up over time. Perhaps your dad taught you - as mine did - that when it comes to real estate, they're just not making much of it anymore - so it will always increase in value.

It's true. When we have a fixed quantity of something (real estate) and a growing demand (more people needing a place to live, work, or play), prices will rise. But our friends at the government have introduced artificial influences that disrupt the supply/demand equation - and the impact of their meddling imposes a direct and significant cost on those of us who own real estate.

I'm going to interview myself here as a way of offering my perspective on the whole real estate valuation issue. If I come close to sounding political here - I apologize - facts are facts.

Question: Home values are down - why?
Answer: Because the "easy-money" lending policies of the early and mid-2000's let too many people into the market for homes they really couldn't afford - and that surge of new buyers (demand) drove prices up.

Question: Why didn't prices stay up?
Answer: Because too many people defaulted on these "sub-prime" mortgages, leading to foreclosures, which has led to a glut of inventory (houses on the market) - much of which is being sold at fire-sale prices by the banks that own them. Now there's more supply than demand - and that drives prices down.

Question: Why did so many people default?
Answer: Because banks lowered their lending standards and gave money to people who had little likelihood of paying it back.

Question: Is that what people mean when they talk about "greedy bankers" - they just lowered their standards to get more loans and collect more fees?
Answer: Yes - but it's really not the bank's fault.

Question: What do you mean?
Answer: Banks have been around for hundreds of years and they didn't wake up stupid one day and forget how to properly underwrite (assess the risk) a home mortgage loan. They lowered their lending standards because our government offered to take on most of the risk of non-payment.

Question: How so?
Answer: Fannie Mae - and Freddie Mac. These are both quasi-government agencies, meaning they're too big to fail, and therefore have access to government money. They told the banks, *"we'll buy your home mortgage loans from you as long as you base your loans on these minimum (lower) set of standards."* The standards were far lower than what banks would loan money out on their own - when they were shouldering the whole risk - "but what the heck - if the government will back us up - take our risk, why not?" "If we don't, we'll get eaten by all the other banks that are lending on these artificially low standards."

Question: Why would Fannie Mae and Freddie Mac agree to guarantee bank loans made on lower lending criteria?

Answer: Because their primary goal was widespread home ownership. They're not bankers - they're politicians - and one measure of their "success" is how many Americans are "prospering" - even if that means creating artificial definitions of *prospering*.

Question: How much of the market did these sub-prime mortgages represent?
Answer: By the government's own estimates - about 40% of all mortgages were sub-prime at the peak.

Question: Have they seen the error of their ways?
Answer: Sort of. There are still Fannie Mae and Freddie Mac lending standards that are below what traditional, prudent banking standards would otherwise permit, but they're higher than they were in the wild-wild west days of mid-decade.

Question: So is a recovery in home prices on the horizon?

Answer: In my opinion, maybe - but on the *distant* horizon. Let's set aside whether we've hit bottom or not yet. I would argue we haven't, but in some respects, it doesn't matter. We're left with a market that has a huge excess of inventory (homes). Many of those homes were bought by people who couldn't afford them. Now - all that inventory is out there (supply), and no more sub-prime loans means that the universe of buyers (who drive the demand) has shrunk by a roughly equal degree. When demand is cut by 40%, and supply is at an all time high, you have a recipe for lower long-term pricing.

Question: *What about people who didn't default - who pay their mortgages?*
Answer: Many of them are "under-water" meaning the value of their home is lower than 1) what they bought it for or 2) what they borrowed against it. That creates a moral hazard - when the financial incentive is to walk away because they owe more than it's worth. Most won't - because they still need a place to live, and most people are honest and believe they must pay what they borrowed, but that's part of the reason I'm not sure we've hit bottom yet. Besides, people may be able to live in a home that they paid $200,000 for even if it's only now worth $150,000 - but they're sure not anxious to sell. That further suppresses real estate transaction activity - the hallmark of demand.

Question: *So when do you think we'll see home prices rebound?*
Answer: They're rebounding now - but in many markets - they have a long way to go to reach full recovery. When we think about the whole supply and demand equation, new demand starts when a renter decides to become a homeowner. For the most part, that means younger people. How are younger people doing in this economy? They suffer the highest unemployment rate - and employment income is the key driver of rational lending. That means many can't qualify. And if they don't buy someone's starter home, the person in that home can't upgrade - so the luxury homes don't move either - which means their values remain stagnant. I hate to be a doomsayer, but I think it could be most of a generation before home prices fully recover to their pre-2008 levels.

Remember - don't shoot the messenger. This is just my opinion - and one of the few times I've chosen to interject it into the dialogue. But we're a full 5 years into the burst bubble, which is nearly a full 1/4 of a generation already - and home values in most parts of the country have seen little improvement. Sure - there are pockets of improvement - but supply and demand don't lie - and they have to resume natural equilibrium before full, across-the-board home values can rise consistently. Remember, if a home's value fell 20% from $100,000 to $80,000 - it must now grow 25% just to get back to even ($80,000 X 125% = $100,000).

Getting back to our regularly scheduled program, we still have the first part of the myth to deal with; that in a market where home values are increasing; having equity is a good investment. Here's my controversial - bold statement that may cause you to bristle before you read the explanation:

Home Equity has a return on investment of exactly zero - I don't care what's happening to real estate values.

Let me explain by way of example. Jill owns a beautiful home that, last year, was valued at $200,000. Good news - Jill's realtor-friend has told Jill that her home increased in value by 5% in the last year, and is now worth $210,000. Jill is thrilled, proudly claiming that her home's equity grew by 5%.

Jack's house is right next door - well actually it's up a small hill (Get it? A little author-humor). His home is identical to Jill's in every way; so it too was worth $200,000 last year - and therefore it too went up 5% in value this year. The difference is that Jack has no equity in his home. In fact, Jack is a sub-prime borrower who borrowed $230,000 to buy the home, and has somehow managed to keep his payments up. His equity - even with the nice 5% rise in home values, is ($20,000). The $10,000 increase in his home's value isn't a "return on his equity," and neither is Jill's - it's appreciation of *the asset* - regardless of equity.

You see, it's the asset that went up in value - not the equity. The asset is the home - not the equity. In fact, equity in a home is just like cash stuffed in a mattress - it can't go up in value. Rather, it goes down in real value by the rate of inflation; and in opportunity value by the rate at which it could otherwise be growing in value if deployed in another asset.

Like it or not, the fact is - equity is dead money. It's no different - literally - than money buried in a hole. It may make Jill sleep better knowing she doesn't have a mortgage payment, but that's only because Jill is oblivious to the liquidity risk she's unwittingly taken on in its place.

We've been taught that Mortgage = Risk; and Free-and-Clear = No risk. Remember, the whole premise of this book is that *"Conventional Wisdom is Often Neither."* Here is a clear example.

This is the myth of home ownership. Am I saying not to own a home? Of course not. What I am saying is that we have to be realistic and look at our homes more the way we look at our cars - as something we need and want in life - not a supplemental wealth account we'll automatically profit from someday.

What I *am* saying is that a home is the most emotional investment we make. When talking about it as a financial asset however, it requires that we set aside emotion, and look at it as a cold, hard financial asset if we're to make good decisions.

Rigged

Part IV - Building Your Fortune

"The significant problems we face cannot be solved at the same level of thinking we were at when we created them."

— *Albert Einstein*

Rigged

Chapter 19

Risk-Free

Buckle up - we're about to begin revealing the secret wealth building strategy all your reading up to now has been leading up to.

Albert Einstein called *compounding interest* the ninth wonder of the world - this may be the tenth!

When we talked about a defensive strategy in Part II of this book, we focused on the three things that erode wealth; market risk, taxes, and investment fees/commissions. As we begin our big reveal, I want to follow the same pattern so you can best evaluate the plan I recommend and understand exactly why it is so powerful.

So let's start with how we grow money without market risk. We said earlier that risk-free exists in the mainstream investing world - but it is almost always associated with dismal returns that won't get us where we want to be with our money. We agreed that safety without a good return is a bit like treading water - we may not drown - but we won't get anywhere either.

So if we're going to eliminate risk, we need to do so while still positioning our money to grow at a competitive rate of return. Therefore, we can't talk "defense" in a vacuum - we have to back up our defense with a strong offensive strategy. If defense alone would suffice, we'd stuff it in a mattress and call it a day - risk eliminated. Instead, this chapter will cover both at the same time. We're going to learn how to eliminate risk - WHILE growing our money at a *very* competitive rate.

For starters, our strategy is not an investment at all, which is why throughout, I've referred to it as a wealth building plan rather than an investment. But if it's not an investment, what is it? It is actually *a money contract*. Now you may have never heard the term "money contract" before - and for good reason - most mainstreamers don't sell money contracts - they sell investments. Money contracts however, are the way we lock in our defensive game plan while starting down the road toward growing our money.

So what is a money contract? As the name suggests, there are certain institutions that will offer us a contractually guaranteed (or at least a contractually defined) outcome for money we put "under contract." The simplest example of a money contract is a bank CD - Certificate of Deposit. When we put money into a CD money contract (the Certificate), our side of the contract says that we'll leave the money in for a certain period of time. The bank's side of the contract promises to pay us a certain rate of interest on our deposit.

That's a contract. In legal terms, there is an **offer** (the certificate itself), **consideration** (our commitment of money - their commitment of interest), and **acceptance** (the purchase transaction in which we exchange money for a contract).

Fortunately, money contracts are not the exclusive domain of banks - so - we're not always relegated to CD-like rates of return. Most of the money contracts I'll show you will pay fixed rates of 4% or more. That's several-fold what bank CD's are paying as of this writing, and for many, will be a very acceptable rate of return - particularly - as we'll learn in the next chapter - since those rates are tax-free. But for most - especially those in the accumulation phase of life - a 4% return is not enough to get you excited.

Fortunately, not every money contract is restricted to a fixed rate of return as is the case of bank CDs. Some have a defined outcome instead. A defined outcome money contract doesn't use a fixed-rate of return. It does offer a guaranteed return, but instead of guaranteeing a stated rate of interest, the contract guarantees (via a definition) *how* the return will be calculated.

An example would be government bonds known as TIPS - Treasury Inflation Protected Securities. These guarantee the bondholder that the interest paid on the bond will be tied to the rate of inflation. In the case of TIPS, we *don't want a fixed rate* like 4% on our money. Rather we want *a guaranteed, contractually defined outcome* - such as an interest rate that will be indexed for inflation. That way, if inflation causes the TIPS rate to go above 4%, we get the benefit of a higher "defined" interest rate, rather than the lower "fixed" interest rate. Whether we choose a fixed rate money contract, or a defined outcome money contract, the important feature to note is that a money contract is the polar opposite of an investment.

An investment is a commitment of money on our part with no guarantee whatsoever. We may "hope" for a certain outcome, but neither the issuer nor the broker, nor the market, gives us the assurance of *any* particular outcome. It is speculative, and we make our decision to invest (or not invest) on a variety of mostly subjective criteria. How stable is the company? What track record does the management team have? What new products are in their pipeline? What is likely to be the future demand for their products? How have they performed in the past? Stated another way:

- ***Investments hope for an outcome by taking images from the rearview mirror, and projecting them into the future.***
- ***Money Contracts are unconcerned with the past, and focus only on defined future deliverables.***

If we're to be about winning the game, and doing so without losing any money along the way, we must have results, not empty promises, educated guesses, or even reasoned hope. In other words, not the kind of stuff we get from mainstream advisors. An investment house or financial advisor cannot – no matter how articulately they may try to convince you otherwise – guarantee results. To do so would be to enter into a contract – *something that by law, they cannot do.*

Let me share one other thought to emphasize the point. What does every commercial investment pamphlet, brochure, order, circular, offering, email, and nearly every other correspondence from a mainstream investment house or advisor say?

"Past results are no guarantee of future performance."

Or something similar. We gloss over this caveat, but it really sums up the whole discussion. They offer nothing other than their best efforts. Their best efforts often turn out to be good enough for some – but they can also disappoint - so they're simply *not* good enough to satisfy our rule set that dictates that *"Failure is not an Option,"* and *"First, Lose No Money."*

So what kind of money contract do we want - and how do we get it?

You'll remember earlier when I agreed that the stock market is the best - or certainly among the best ways to grow our money. Unfortunately, played the way most of us play it, it's also the best way to lose money quickly. That's because most of us assume all the downside risk of a stock or a stock market when we put money in.

Remember our friend Thurston Howell, III? He bought bonds that paid a certain rate and then invested the interest he was *guaranteed* on those bonds - into stock or stock options. That way, if the stock goes into the tank, Mr. Howell is protected. If it soars - he gets all the upside. In that chapter, we determined that most of us couldn't play the game the way Mr. Howell does, because we wouldn't be able to grow our limited amount of money fast enough to build real wealth.

Well it turns out - there is a way to play the game like Thurston Howell - and like Warren Buffett - a way that doesn't *manage* the risk - but *eliminates* it. It's called **equity-linked indexing**, and you won't find it at your broker's office.

To begin the discussion of equity-linked indexing, let's lay some groundwork. There are only three ways any investment can move; up, down, or sideways. If you were told you could eliminate one of these outcomes but had to live with the other two, which would you choose to eliminate?

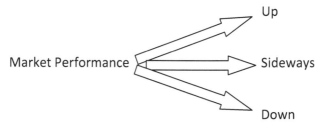

Obviously, we would choose to eliminate the downside risk. That would fit our rule - Lose No Money. It would also mean we could participate in the upside of the market, so we wouldn't be relegated to the low returns of other so-called low, and no-risk investments.

The key feature of equity-linked indexing is that it does exactly that - it eliminates the possibility of downside risk to our principal, while permitting us to capture much of the upside potential of the stock market. That way, if the market takes a dive, our principal and all locked in gains are completely, 100% protected from *any* downward movement. Money contracts call this minimum earnings rate, the "floor" rate. The floor rate in a money contract will never be less than zero - no gain-no loss. But some money contracts have floor rates that guarantee growth of up to 3% (in the current environment).

In exchange for that downside protection, money contracts also set a "cap" on earnings that will be credited to our money contract account balance. In a big year when the actual performance of the market index exceeds the cap, our upside may be limited to the cap rate. Different money contracts have different cap rates, but in the current environment, caps range from about 10% all the way up to 17%.

The market or "index" to which the guarantees apply can be almost anything. The most common is the S&P 500 index. It is among the oldest and broadest of stock market indices, and is generally regarded as the best overall indicator of corporate performance among publicly traded companies.

For purposes of this discussion, let's look at a money contract with a 2% floor, and a 12% cap, tied to the S&P 500 Stock Market Index. Here's how the money in a money contract would perform:

- If the S&P goes down or grows at less than 2% in any given year - our money contract balance would grow by the floor rate of 2%.

- If the S&P goes up by more than 12% in any given year, our money contract balance would grow by the cap rate of 12%.

- If the S&P goes up by 8.26% in a given year, the balance in our money contract would grow by exactly 8.26% since that falls between the 2% floor rate and the 12% cap rate.

The floors and caps result in a "range" of outcomes that the money contract can generate. The range is widest when the floor is zero, and narrows as the floor is raised. For example, in the current money contract environment, if the floor is zero, the cap might be 14%, providing a 14% range. If the floor is 2%, the cap might be 12%, resulting in a 10% range - and so on.

Which "range" is best? There is no scientific answer, but in my opinion, the wider the range, the better the outcome will be. So given the choice of a 2% & 12% range and a 0% &14% range, I would personally tend to choose the latter. In some markets, the 2% & 12% money contract can work out better. And since many people would prefer to see *some* growth each year, the 2% floor rate may be preferable. But in general, I believe the widest range of outcomes will produce the best result overall.

Let's start to examine how a money contract with a floor and cap might work in actual practice. Based on what you've learned so far - what does your instinct tell you your outcome would be with an equity-indexed money contract offering a 2% floor and a 12% cap - when compared to the actual performance of the overall market itself? Would a "floor and cap" money contract perform better than the market, worse than the market, or about the same as the market?

Let's find out. First, we'll look at the market itself. The chart below looks at the S&P 500 stock market index performance over the last 100 years - from 1911 through 2011. The bars represent the percentage rate of growth (or contraction) in the market each year.

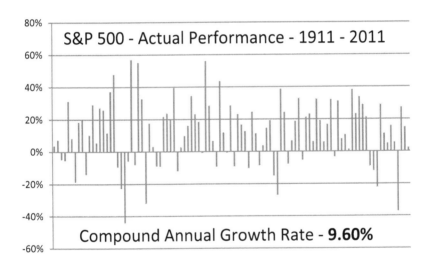

The first, and most important figure to pay attention to is the Compound Annual Growth rate, which, for this index (the S&P 500) over this time period (100 years), was 9.60%. As we learned in an earlier chapter, the CAGR tells us what would have actually happened to our money. Now 9.6% is a good rate of return - most of us would probably take that over an investing lifetime and call it a day. The problem is, most of us don't have an accumulation phase that spans 100 years. So our 30-40 year window could result in a figure that is much different than this. That difference will be more a result of how many down years creep into our accumulation phase - than how good the good years are. Therein lies the power of equity indexing with an earnings floor/downside protection.

As it turns out, the market produced a negative return, or a return of less than 2% in 29 of the last 100 years. In an equity-indexed money contract, our money would have grown in each of those years by exactly 2%. On the other hand, precisely 50 of those 100 years had returns that exceeded 12%. In those years, we would not have realized the full market's gain because our cap rate would have limited our growth to 12%. At first blush, it may seem that what we *give up* in the 50 years wouldn't be worth what we *gain* in 29 years. Let's see. First, let's look at what would happen if we just applied the 2% floor without the cap.

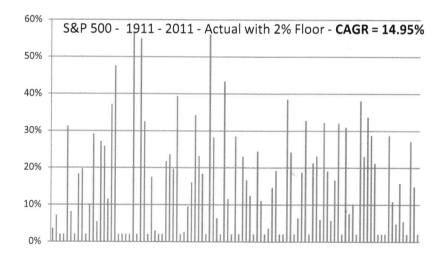

Wow. Could you imagine that just by changing those 29 losing years to +2% gain years (leaving everything else the same), the Compound Annual Growth Rate catapults from 9.6%, all the way up to 14.95%? That's an improvement of over 50% just by eliminating the stinkers. If you grasped what we meant when we talked about the devastation of losses way back in Chapter 5, you now know why Einstein got so excited about the idea of compound interest that he called it the Ninth Wonder of the World. You see, there is no compounding when a string of growth is interrupted by a loss - and now we see it on display.

It would be great if we could get the 2% floor without a cap as this chart shows, but we can't. In order to get the protection of the floor, we have to accept the limitation of the cap. The chart below shows what happens when we lay the cap on top of the floor underneath.

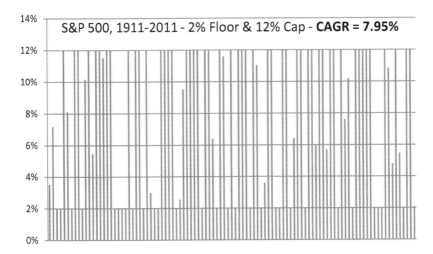

Now - each year shows a minimum of 2% growth, a maximum of 12% growth, or the actual market result when it falls between the floor and the cap. The net result is a CAGR of 7.95%.

Not bad - but also not quite as good as the market itself would have performed, which we learned earlier was 9.6%. Every time period we might choose will have a different outcome. Sometimes, the floor and cap strategy will actually out-perform the overall market, and sometimes, like in our example here, it will not. But by using a 100-year period of time, I can't be accused of cherry-picking a period that might favor a money contract over the market itself since - over this 100-year period - it does not.

In our 100-year analysis, the "cost of safety" (the difference between the market's 9.6% return and our equity-indexed return of 7.95%), is a 1.65% difference.

Now there are three very important points to make here.

- First, what would have happened if we had chosen a money contract with a zero percent floor, and a 14% cap instead? Over the same 100-year period, we would have achieved a CAGR of **8.26%** - slightly better than the 7.95% we got using the 2% floor and 12% cap rate we explored earlier. That lowers the "safety" cost to 1.34%.

- Even if safety means we accept a discount to the market itself - whether its 1.65%, 1.34%, or some other number (and remember - sometimes it will be a "safety premium" depending on the time period selected), we need to consider the peace of mind we'd have knowing that even in a 2008 disaster, our account balance is actually growing by 2%. It's hard to measure the value of peace of mind, but ask yourself this question. In 2008, were you calm, cool, and collected - convinced that the market would come back in a reasonable period of time? Or, were you panicked - pulling money out - or tempted to do so - comforted little by your broker/advisor's assurances that things would come back? When rolling the dice on the market over 40-50-or 60 years, there can be a lot of sleepless nights when markets are uncooperative. Would you rather endure them, or eliminate them for a small cost in your overall return?

- Finally, what if we could get an equity-indexed CAGR in the 8% range that was tax-free? I've been hinting all along that a tax-free money contract is entirely possible. But for the moment, let's do a bit more math. If we could achieve the overall market CAGR of 9.6%, we'd have to pay taxes on the growth. Those taxes would leave us with a net, after-tax CAGR. The chart below shows how our 7.95% CAGR (a money contract with a floor and cap of 2% and 12%) - and our 8.26% CAGR (a money contract with a floor and cap of 0% and 14%) would stack up after taking taxes away from the market's actual CAGR of 9.6%.

	Tax-Adjusted Actual CAGR	CAGR - Equity Indexed, 2%/12%	Tax-Adjusted Risk Premium	CAGR - Equity Indexed, 0%/14%	Tax-Adjusted Risk Premium
Before taxes	9.60%	7.95%	-1.65%	8.26%	-1.34%
20% Tax Rate	7.68%	7.95%	+.27%	8.26%	+.58%
30%Tax Rate	6.72%	7.95%	+1.03%	8.26%	+1.54%
40% Tax Rate	5.76%	7.95%	+2.01%	8.26%	+1.50%

Under any reasonable tax scenario, a tax-free equity-indexed money contract will actually out-perform the market itself - often by 1% or more. In the chapter on fees and commissions, we learned that a 1% fee can mean 28% less money in retirement - so it stands to reason that

1% of additional return on investment can likewise increase our cash at retirement by the same 28%. In other words, the risk-elimination cost may turn out to be a risk-premium that can turbo-charge our cash accumulation.

There's another - less obvious feature of equity indexing that bears mention. Each time earnings are credited to our money contract account (usually annually or monthly); those earnings are subject to the same guarantee against loss going forward that our original principal is protected by. So not only can we never lose a penny of our principal, *we can never lose a penny of gains* that have been credited to our account.

I like to think of it as an imaginary "Never Below" lever. Each time earnings are posted to our account, we can move our "Never Below" lever up underneath our new (higher) balance with the certainty that in fact we'll never have less money than we do at that very point - even if markets crash tomorrow.

One last point. I'm often asked how the issuer of a money contract can deliver the kinds of guarantees we've been looking at here. At times, it can seem almost too good to be true, so the question of credibility comes up often.

The short answer to the question is that the money contract issuer uses a combination of bond discounts and stock market options to achieve the equity-indexed outcome. While *we* take no market risk as the contract owner, it is interesting to note that the contract issuer takes no market risk either - and that's why it's <u>not</u> too good to be true.

To answer the question more precisely, we have to go beyond "what time is it" to "how is the watch made?" The following discussion is from Jim Bergstrom, a Certified Financial Analyst. His paper does a good job of explaining exactly how a money contract issuer can offer an equity-indexed floor and cap money contract without assuming investment risk themselves.

> *Equity-indexed products are comprised of three main elements: a "call option" <u>purchased</u> by the issuer, a "call option" <u>sold</u> by the issuer, and "<u>general account</u>."*
>
> *Call options give an investor the right (but not the obligation), to buy something at a predetermined price at a specific date in the future. Let's say you think the S&P 500 is going to do well over*

the next year, but don't want to take the risk of owning it and seeing its value decline significantly if you're wrong.

Instead of buying the S&P 500 Index near its current value of, say 900, you buy a call option for $100 that gives you the right (but not the obligation) to buy the S&P 500 a year from now at a value of 900.

So if the S&P 500 is at 1200 a year from now, you'd exercise your right to buy it for 900. You would receive $300 next June or a net of $200 net after paying the $100 cost of the option.

If the S&P 500 crashes further and goes down to 600, you wouldn't exercise your right to buy it for 900. You'd be out your $100, but would avoid the $300 loss that would have occurred if you had instead owned the index outright. This is where the downside protection comes in.

For investors seeking to avoid losses, call options are great tools. The problem, though, is that the cost of the option is pretty high. A $100 cost when the S&P 500 is at a value of 900 is 11%. So if the market is flat over the next year, the investor would lose 11%.

One way to reduce that loss is to sell a call option at a higher price, and effectively sell part of the potential upside to someone else. For example, you could sell a call option that gives someone else the right to buy the S&P 500 at a value of 1000 a year from now. The buyer of that option would pay you $55. That reduces the combined cost of both options to $45, or 4.5%.

If you have a $90,000 equity-indexed contract, that means the issuer would pay roughly $10,000 to buy the call option, and receive $5,500 for selling the call option. The net cost is $4,500.

The issuer then invests the remaining $85,500 as part of its "general account" with the intention of growing it safely, to be worth about $90,000 a year from now. When they do so successfully, the net money contract return depends on what level the S&P 500 closes at a year from now (the option value).

If the S&P 500 is worth 950 a year from now, the first call option - the one the insurer bought - will result in a $5,000 gain. The second call option - the one the insurer sold - expires worthless, *since the S&P isn't above 1000. So the contract owner's account is now worth $95,000 ($90,000 plus $5,000), and realizes a gain of $5,000 – a bit more than 5%.*

If the S&P 500 crashes to 600, neither option is exercised, and the contract is still worth $90,000 – right where it started.

If the S&P 500 soars to 1200, the issuer receives $30,000 for the purchased call option, but has to pay $20,000 to the owner of the second call. Net, the issuer receives $10,000 and the contract owner's account is worth $100,000 – a nice gain of just over 10%.

If the S&P 500 doubles to 1800, the issuer receives $90,000 for the purchased option but has to pay $80,000 to the owner of the second. Again, the net is $10,000 received. Any level for the S&P that is above 1000 results in a $10,000 gain – no more, no less – thus the "capped" gain of about 10% for the money contract owner.

Not every equity-indexing strategy purchases and sells the call options at exactly the levels shown in Bergstrom's example. Some might be higher or lower – and produce a greater or lesser upside cap. It will depend largely on what the contract specifies. Nonetheless, the illustration is enlightening and shows how those who issue equity-indexed contracts achieve their results.

Finally, as you get into the world of equity-indexed money contracts, you'll discover that the industry does a good job of making it as confusing as possible. They do this in two ways. First, they offer different kinds of growth crediting options that introduce terms like "spread" and "participation rate." The insert below attempts to simplify them. Additionally, a variety of market indices are used - and sometimes blended. The insert also comments on those.

> Money contracts come in all shapes, sizes, and varieties. The common characteristic among them all, is that there is an earnings range that provides downside protection and an upside cap of some sort. The generic term used by the money-contract industry to describe how earnings will be credited to the money contract, is the "crediting method."

Another way of imposing an earnings limitation is through a "participation" rate. With a participation rate money contract, there will be a floor, but not a *fixed* cap. Instead, the money contract owner will "participate" in a pre-determined portion of the market's gain - for example - 70%. Participation rate contracts technically have no cap, which is their appeal. Consider a year when the index grows by 40%. In a contract with a 70% participation rate (some are higher, some are lower), the contract owner would be credited with 28% growth that year (70% X 40%). The difference between 70% and 100% represents the margin retained by the contract issuer.

A third crediting method is called the "spread." A spread is similar to the participation rate in that it creates a way for the contract issuer to retain a portion of the earnings. A typical spread might be 2%. Therefore, the owner of a spread-type contract would get the market return less 2%. So in a 5% up market, the owner would be credited with 3% - and in a 50% up market - with 48%.

Just to confuse matters, sometimes earnings are credited using a combination - for example, a spread with a hard cap; a participation rate with a hard cap, and so on. Regardless, the floor will never be less than zero - which is the most important feature.

One other feature worth knowing about money contracts is that the index to which the crediting method is tied, can be almost anything - or even a blend of anything. In our earlier example, we talked about a floor and cap crediting method tied to the S&P 500 Stock Index. But we could just as easily have chosen a money contract whose performance is linked to the NASDAQ, the Heng Seng, or many others. Sometimes, a money contract issuer will even offer a weighted blend of indexes, i.e. 40% S&P 500, 40% EuroStoxx, and 20% Nikkei.

Here's my personal commentary about all these derivations. They exist because there are investors (and advisors) who believe they have insights that will lead them to conclude that one crediting method - or one index - will outperform another. This variety comes at the cost of confusing the average investor. In my view - if all the various indexes and crediting methods were plotted on a graph over a 20 year - or so - timeframe, I seriously doubt there would be a significant long-term performance difference among any of them.

I want this concept to really sink in - and I want you to be able to look at it from different angles so you can see its power, and believe in its potential. So the following table looks at what would have happened to our money if we had put $100,000 into an equity-indexed money contract between 1976 and 2011 - a 35-year window - and left it there for 20 years. The chart looks at each 20-year segment (i.e. 1991-2001, 1986-2006, etc.) and identified the *worst* day to have placed our money into that 20-year money contract, the *best* day, and the *mid-point* day.

20 - Year Periods from 1975 - 2011

Duration	Worst 1/6/1992		Middle 11/16/1990		Best 4/6/1980	
	Account Value	Annualized Return	Account Value	Annualized Return	Account Value	Annualized Return
0	$100,000	N/A	$100,000	N/A	$100,000	N/A
1	$103,962	3.96%	$112,000	12.00%	$112,000	12.00%
2	$111,762	7.50%	$123,141	9.95%	$114,240	2.00%
3	$113,997	2.00%	$136,623	10.95%	$127,949	12.00%
4	$127,677	12.00%	$139,356	2.00%	$131,710	2.94%
5	$142,998	12.00%	$156,079	12.00%	$147,515	12.00%
6	$160,158	12.00%	$174,808	12.00%	$165,217	12.00%
7	$179,377	12.00%	$195,785	12.00%	$185,043	12.00%
8	$197,861	10.30%	$219,279	12.00%	$188,744	2.00%
9	$201,818	2.00%	$245,593	12.00%	$209,930	11.22%
10	$205,854	2.00%	$250,505	2.00%	$235,121	12.00%
11	$209,971	2.00%	$255,515	2.00%	$259,513	10.37%
12	$235,168	12.00%	$260,625	2.00%	$280,413	8.05%
13	$248,608	5.72%	$291,900	12.00%	$305,005	8.77%
14	$269,026	8.21%	$326,661	11.91%	$311,105	2.00%
15	$295,032	9.67%	$342,162	4.75%	$348,437	12.00%
16	$300,933	2.00%	$383,222	12.00%	$390,250	12.00%
17	$306,951	2.00%	$399,369	4.21%	$437,080	12.00%
18	$343,786	12.00%	$407,357	2.00%	$489,530	12.00%
19	$385,040	12.00%	$456,239	12.00%	$548,273	12.00%
20	$392,741	2.00%	$484,635	6.22%	$614,066	12.00%

Annualized Rate of Return over term (20 years)	7.08%	8.21%	9.50%

Here's how to interpret the table.

- The worst day to have deposited $100,000 into an equity-indexed money contract in the last 35 years would have been **January 6, 1992**. Had we done so, and allowed our money to compound for the next 20 years under the same equity indexing option, we would have turned $100,000 into **$392,741**, representing a compound annual growth rate (CAGR) of **7.08%**.

- The middle-of-the-road day to have deposited $100,000 into an equity-indexed money contract in the last 35 years would have been **November 16, 1990**. Had we done so, and allowed our money to compound for the next 20 years under the same equity indexing option, we would have turned $100,000 into **$484,635**, representing a compound annual growth rate of **8.21%**.
- The best day to have deposited $100,000 into an equity-indexed money contract in the last 35 years would have been **April 6, 1980**. Had we done so, and allowed our money to compound for the next 20 years under the same equity indexing option, we would have turned $100,000 into **$614,066**, representing a compound annual growth rate of **9.50%**.

I call this the Midas Touch vs. Murphy's Law comparison. If you're one of those people who have bad luck, the worst you would have done had you put it into a equity-indexed money contract in the last 35 years, would have been to quadruple your money, and earn a compound annual return of 7.08%. The best you would have done would be 9.50%. And had you thrown a dart and purchased this money contract at the mid-point, you would have achieved a CAGR of 8.21%. This is very consistent with our analysis at the beginning of the chapter where we showed an equity-indexed return over 100 years of 7.95%.

Here's one final way to look at how we might expect an equity indexing strategy to perform. This chart looks at one-year, and 20-year periods over the last 35 years. It tells us what percentage of one-year periods, and what percentage of 20-year periods; would have achieved a certain CAGR (left-hand column).

>%	1-YEAR PERIODS	20-YEAR PERIODS
4.5%	63.0%	100.0%
5.0%	61.9%	100.0%
5.5%	61.3%	100.0%
6.0%	60.5%	99.7%
6.5%	58.9%	99.0%
7.0%	56.8%	94.4%
7.5%	55.6%	78.0%
8.0%	53.3%	54.9%
8.5%	52.5%	25.2%
9.0%	51.4%	7.7%
9.5%	50.8%	1.0%

As you can see from the table, more than 94% of all 20-year periods would have achieved a compound rate of return of 7% or greater, with one in four (25.2%) reaching an 8.5% CAGR or more. Again considering that those returns are tax-free, you can really begin to appreciate the power of equity indexing as a wealth building strategy.

To close out our discussion of equity indexing, you'll recall that in Chapter nine we talked about all the reasons it's nearly impossible to get the full market return - which is only slightly higher than the figures we've just examined using equity indexing. Let's revisit those reasons and see why equity indexing gives us such a leg up.

Direct Market Investment	Equity-Indexed Market Investing
1. We never "own" the whole market	Equity-Indexing contracts by comparison do "own" the whole market – that's what the index is, whether it's the Dow, the S&P, or another market index
2. We never "capture" the full gains/losses	An equity-indexing strategy locks in gains at a certain point in time. That new "lock" level becomes the beginning principal for the next period so we cannot lose our gains.
3. Returns are eroded by Fees and Commissions	With equity-indexing, there are "fees," but we get the tangible value of downside protection along with some other goodies we'll cover later.
4. Direct market investing is tax-inefficient.	Properly structured, we can use equity-indexing inside a vehicle that will allow us to take our money out - principal and growth - completely income tax free - that's 100%
5. Recovery Time can be devastating depending on your investing timeline	The key feature of equity-indexing is that losses are locked out, so there *is* never a recovery period. And since each period stands on its own, we can often

	capture gains in markets that are in an overall downward cycle.

The point is this: I could introduce you to millions of retirees who - if they had it to do over again - would take any of these equity-indexed outcomes compared to what they did over their investing lifetimes.

Most would have a ton more money - and all of them would have slept a lot better over that time knowing that no matter what happened in the market, their money was not only safe - but chugging away at a good rate of growth.

Rigged

Chapter 20

Tax-Free

Now there's a small chance that a few of you aren't jumping up and down about a growth rate of 7% - 9.5%. I think you're either unrealistically confident, greedy or downright crazy not to get excited about those numbers - but let me sweeten the pot a bit and see if we can't get your heart rate up a bit.

The second of our wealth eroders was taxation. So the second component of our defensive game plan has to be to eliminate the ravages of taxation on our money. In the last chapter, we learned that a money contract rate of return between 7% - 9.5% was not unreasonable - and that some money contracts offered earning caps of up to 17%. If we could achieve those kinds of results on a tax-free basis, 7% would be the mainstream (taxable) equivalent of 10%; and a 9.5% return would be the taxable equivalent of 12.5% (assuming a marginal tax rate of 30%). Does that get you a bit more excited?

We can do exactly that - but to understand how we can immunize our money from taxes, we have to think in ways that are foreign to the mainstreamers.

So let's say over the years, we've successfully built a $1,000,000 balance in our money contract account and now - rather than putting more in - we're at the stage in life where we want our money contract account to start paying us a retirement income. If we start taking money out of the money contract, all the earnings are taxable just as they would be in any other investment vehicle or investment account. That's how the mainstream world works - and in that regard, there is nothing special about our money contract that exempts its earning from taxation.

The difference is that the money contract issuer - the financial institution that established the money contract in the first place - will allow us to borrow money *from* them, since we have a money contract balance *with* them. Our money contract is not "collateral" in the traditional sense of the word; rather it acts as what bankers call a "compensating balance." In other words, while the money contract balance is not formally pledged against any loans we may take, its mere presence is an inducement for the money contract issuer to offer this loan option.

The reason this is so significant, is that borrowed money (money that is not ours) is not income - and therefore is not taxable. This is *very* important to understand. **Loans from the money contract issuer do not come out of our money contract account** - they come from the issuer's account.

Our money contract balance is still ours - 100% of it. That means, it continues to grow on the very same terms of the contract that existed from day one. So while we're borrowing money from the issuer to create a retirement income stream, 100% of the money in our money contract account continues to grow - not 100% minus whatever we've taken out as income. Let me repeat - 100% of our money contract balance continues to grow according to the terms of the money contract.

Why go to the trouble of borrowing money instead of just withdrawing money from our money contract account? The answer is that **loans aren't taxable**. There is no tax when we take out a mortgage. There is no tax when we borrow money to finance the purchase of a car. And there is no tax when we borrow money by charging a purchase to a credit card.

So if we can borrow, rather than invading our money contract account, we've just found a way to get at money tax-free. It doesn't matter that it's not our money - that's a technicality. If we didn't have a money contract balance, we couldn't borrow in the first place - so it has the same effect as getting at our own money - except that we skip the part where a direct withdrawal of our own money would create a taxable event.

There is a similar provision in the mainstream world that you may be familiar with. It's called a "margin loan." If we had a taxable investment account with most of the big Wall Street firms, we could borrow money from them *against* the balance in our investment account - at least a portion of it. Aggressive investors will take advantage of this option to create more capital to invest. That's great when markets are moving up. But when markets move against the investor, it can trigger another term that is more familiar to us - a "margin call." In a margin call situation, the lender (Wall Street firm) requires that the investor put additional capital into their account to cover the lender's loan risk.

There are several differences between loans from a money contract issuer - and margin loans made by a Wall Street firm. The most significant of which is that a margin loan is directly collateralized by the investment account. That's why - if the investment account loses value - there can be a margin call. The lender is essentially saying there is insufficient collateral to secure their loan principal.

Another significant difference is that eventually, a margin loan has to be repaid - with interest. As we'll learn in a moment, we have an option in our money contract scenario that will eliminate the necessity of any repayment - I know - sounds too good to be true again - but hang with me.

I'm sure your mind is racing ahead - and you have questions about this whole line of thinking:

1. Don't I have to make loan payments that would wipe out the tax-free benefit of the money I borrowed in the first place?

2. Won't the lender charge interest on the borrowed money?

3. If there is an interest charge - where will that money come from?

4. At some point - won't I have to take money out of my money contract account - and if so - won't the earnings be taxed eventually anyway?

Those are all great questions. And if we confine the answers to what we know about borrowing money in the mainstream world - the answers would all be YES - and they would make this entire discussion a pointless mental exercise.

But we're not in mainstream-land anymore - just like Dorothy is not in Kansas anymore. And here's where our money contract issuer does us a fourth - huge favor. If you're keeping score at home, here's what the money contract issuer has already offered us:

1. We're offered a guarantee of no principal loss to any of the money we put into our money contract, plus any earnings that are credited to our money contract account.

2. We're offered a growth rate that is either fixed (at a rate that is higher than any other fixed, guaranteed instrument), or equity-indexed, which gives us the upside of the market; and combined, may actually allow us to earn more than the market itself would yield.

3. Because we have a money contract account balance with the issuer, they offer to loan us *their own money*; which we can use as an income stream, for life events - or for any other purpose.

The fourth huge favor the money contract issuer does, is to let us both collateralize and **repay our loan with the proceeds from a life insurance policy**. By putting a life insurance policy in place and making the money contract issuer a partial beneficiary, we shift the collateral burden off of our money contract balance, and onto the insurance policy - 100%. And because we can buy so many future dollars for so few today dollars through a life insurance policy, we can very easily and inexpensively cover repayment of both the principal and the interest on the loan(s).

Let's go back to our questions from a few minutes ago - and see exactly how this works.

- *Don't I have to make loan payments that would wipe out the tax-free benefit of the money I borrowed in the first place?* With a life insurance policy in place, the lender doesn't require loan payments during our lifetime. Instead, he just keeps a ledger of what we owe. So the answer to the first question is NO - we don't have to make payments along the way.

- *Won't the lender charge interest on the borrowed money?* Yes - there is an interest charge. Every month, the lender keeps track of what we owe - adds any additional amount we may have borrowed that month, plus an interest charge for the month on the new total. But since he doesn't require a payment - he just writes it in the ledger book and keeps track of the running total.

- *If there is an interest charge - where will that money come from?* The accrued balance in the lender's ledger will be repaid from the proceeds of the life insurance policy at death. You see, our lender is very patient. He doesn't care so much *when* he gets repaid - only that he *does* get repaid. So for him, life insurance is a perfectly acceptable solution to his repayment issue. The likelihood of him getting repaid is 100% - because as much as we may want to deny it - we are going to die at some point, and that life insurance benefit will wipe our slate clean. So with the money to repay the loan balance coming from a life insurance policy, we're left with one more question.

- **_Won't I have to take money from my money contract account at some point - and pay taxes on the growth in that account?_** And here - the lender does us a *fifth* huge favor. The lender says that as long as we have that life insurance policy, when we die, they'll just take the money contract balance, call it even - and give our estate all of the remaining life insurance death benefit money instead.

Why is that such a big favor? Three gigantic reasons:

- First, the life insurance benefit will ALWAYS be greater than the money contract account balance, *and* greater than the loan ledger balance (including interest) - so our heirs <u>will get more money from the life insurance proceeds than they would have, had they inherited our money contract account balance instead</u>.
- Second, if we (or our heirs) never have to take possession of the money in our money contract, no tax event is triggered - to them - or us - ever.
- Third, life insurance death benefits are - by law - income tax free. So net, net - our heirs get more money than we built or that remains in our money contract account - and we've legally avoided paying taxes on a lifetime of wealth we've built because they will receive it as a life insurance benefit.

Do you see the power - the magic - of this approach? Are you beginning to see that we can use this strategy to build truly tax-free wealth that we can access tax-free *and* pass on tax-free? Just how far ahead of everyone else on your block would you be with a wealth building strategy like this? Taxes take a huge bite out of most people's wealth - and we just discovered a way to opt out entirely - with the blessing of federal and state taxing authorities - including the IRS.

Now I know we just answered a bunch of really good - really tough questions. But in doing so - we've raised a couple more.

- Life insurance isn't free - so didn't we just introduce a new layer of cost to this whole thing?

- Is there really a lender out there that offers terms like we've just described? And if so - what are the qualifications we have to meet in order to borrow money from them?

The fact is - we *did* just introduce a new layer of cost, because it is true - life insurance isn't free. But there are a few important points we need to consider.

- First, pure life insurance is incredibly inexpensive. If we're given the choice of paying an insurance premium for the rest of our lives - versus paying taxes the rest of our lives - I can assure you the insurance premiums will be a small fraction of what the taxes would have been over that same lifetime.

- Besides, we know from the very first pages of this book that we need life insurance anyway - so there really is no "additional" cost, and now, we've discovered a second use for that life insurance that gives us a gigantic living benefit - **NO TAXES** - ever.

- Finally, the cost we do incur for the life insurance is going to be refunded to our estate in the form of that portion of the death benefit that exceeds our loan balance. So in a very real sense, the cost of insurance in the end will be zero. I'll take that deal seven days a week and twice on Sunday. How about you?

But there's even more good news. Remember that in the scenario we just painted, our money contract money is 100% intact - earning more money for us every day - even as we borrow money from the lender to support our lifestyle needs. If everybody else on the block built their wealth the mainstream way - and started out with the same pot of wealth and took the same amount out each month - their account balance is going down by what they draw from it - and up by what (if anything) they earn on it.

Ours, on the other hand, never goes down - it only goes up - because we're not drawing anything from it. That means the earnings on the additional money we keep in our money contract account pays for some - maybe all - of the cost of the life insurance. Let's look at it this way:

	Bob the Mainstreamer	Jill the "*Rigged*" reader
Beg. Balance at retirement	$1,000,000	$1,000,000
Annual Drawdown	$40,000	$40,000 (loan)
Annual Life Ins. Premium	0	$10,000
Net Earning balance	$960,000	$990,000
Earnings (assume 5%)	$48,000	$49,500
Balance at End of Year	$1,008,000	$1,039,500
Difference		+ $31,500

There are three key takeaways from this analysis. The most obvious - the one that leaps off the page, is that even after enduring a $10,000 life insurance premium, Jill ends up with $31,500 more at the end of just one year - a figure that will continue to grow at a compounded rate as time goes on. By the way - I've assumed a $10,000 annual insurance premium - which may be more - or may be less depending on Jill's age and health - but only in the most extreme situations, would she be worse off than Bob - and she would know it before she ever started down this path in the first place.

The second item of note is less obvious. Some of you may have picked up on the fact that Jill did not draw down her account - so it seems she had no money to live on. True - she didn't draw down on her money contract account - but she did borrow $40,000 from her lender, so they had the same *gross income* to live on.

Why do I say "gross" income? Because it's likely that Bob hasn't been taxed yet on the $40,000 he took out of his account. If his $40,000 was all taxable, he lived on about $28,000 after taxes - while Jill lived it up on the full $40,000 *because there are no taxes on borrowed money.*

Finally, since our strategy does involve Jill borrowing her $40,000, there is an interest charge. Now as we said before, that interest is just footnoted in a ledger - she doesn't actually have to pay it - but let's incorporate it into the analysis anyway, to get a real apples-to-apples comparison of the two plans. Let's reduce Jill's account balance by the interest she may owe on the $40,000 she borrowed to live on. At 5% interest, her ledger would show that she owes $42,000 ($40,000 of borrowed principal plus $2,000 of accrued interest) - reducing her lead on Bob from $31,500 - all the way down to $29,500. I'll bet she's still thrilled.

By the way, Jill has the option to pay the interest cost periodically, just not the obligation. In many cases, it may make sense to do so, since the interest charge will likely be less than the tax bill on a similar withdrawal from a mainstream plan. In our example, Jill's accrued interest was $2,000 - while Bob's tax bill may have been $12,000 - or more. Repaying interest will also mean that more of Jill's insurance benefit will pass to her estate.

Before we move on, the one remaining question is what the qualifications are for borrowing from the money contract issuer - and the answer is perhaps the most exciting part of this strategy. Think about it from the lender's point of view. There are two concerns any lender needs to be comfortable with before they'll lend money.

1. **Does the borrower have enough credit/income/reserves to faithfully make payments?**

2. **What collateral will I receive if the borrower fails to repay me?**

To answer the first question, remember that the lender does not *require* any payments. Instead, the lender adds interest to the prior period's balance, and carries it forward - forever. Since payments are not required, the lender's first question is a non-issue - they don't need to worry about the ability to repay.

Here's what that means for you and I. It means that with this lender, there are no applications, qualifications, nosy questions, documentation requirements, etc. None. All we need to do is inform the lender of how much we need, and tell them where to send the check. It doesn't matter if we're out of work, sick, or are enduring any other circumstance or hardship that might cause a mainstream lender to deny a loan request. Those don't apply to us.

We also know the answer to the second question. The collateral for the loan is the life insurance policy. We don't have to pledge the house, the car, or the kids - just the life insurance. So our other assets are not backing up these loans.

A word of caution, however. For the life insurance to serve as collateral - it has to exist - and it exists only with proper care and feeding - meaning premium payments. Now nobody likes paying insurance premiums of any kind. So let's set up our plan so we never have to write a check. By using a portion of the earnings on our money contract account to pay the premiums, there are no checks. We just let the insurance company pull the premium out of our money contract and we're done.

And one final caveat. Sometimes - in a rare, sustained down market (where our money contract is earning zero), there may not be enough earnings in the money contract to pay the insurance premium. Most people will allow the premium to come out of the money contract account anyway - reducing its principal balance. In extremely rare cases, a policy can be in danger of lapsing if it gets close to "consuming" the money contract to support the life insurance premium cost. This is not an outcome we want. Because our money contract balance serves as a secondary source of collateral - it would have to be used to repay the lender for any loans plus interest we may have drawn to date.

And if that happens, we will have "invaded" our money contract balance (something we would never do in ordinary circumstances), and guess what monster comes back to haunt us? That's right, the tax man. All the earnings are taken out of the account, and just like taking money out of any other mainstream investment account, those earnings are taxable.

What we just covered is one of two risks in this whole strategy - the risk that earnings on the money contract is insufficient to cover the cost of the insurance that collateralizes the tax-free loans (plus any additional loans you might require for living expenses).

The second risk is that the insurance company itself fails, jeopardizing the policy that serves in the collateral position. The first risk is real - but rare. The second risk is almost nil - but in the interest of full disclosure, bears mentioning. We'll cover that risk in more detail in a later chapter.

Neither of these risks rise to the level of the principal risk markets impose on mainstream investors every day - and neither risk is tied to the performance of any market. But in the same way we take risk when we get out of bed in the morning - there are risks in this plan - small as they may be - and there you have them.

Rigged

Chapter 21

Fee-Neutral

Now we look at the third of the wealth eroders - fees and commissions. We discussed at length, the devastating effect of fees and commissions on our wealth-building quest over a lifetime, and speculated that - just as we'd have a whole lot better lifestyle without risk and taxes - we'd do even better if we could avoid the fees and commissions.

Well - confession time - we can't. I just acknowledged in the last chapter that there will be a cost of insurance if we use the plan we outlined. Although the cost of insurance isn't a fee or commission in the traditional sense of the word - it does drag our account down - and therefore warrants our attention.

Even though we concluded that the cost of insurance is a more than acceptable tradeoff to get rid of taxes - forever - it's there nonetheless. So if we can't avoid it - let's see if we can neutralize its impact? What do I mean?

Remember that the life insurance death benefit sends a pot of money to our heirs that is greater than the balance of our money contract account on its own will ever be. The difference - that extra money - essentially means that the cost of insurance is refunded to our estate, often at interest! In other words, we get most of it - all of it - or sometimes more than all of it back - in the form of the death benefit that's paid to our estate.

So while we might have to bear the cost during our lifetime, getting it refunded back to our estate is the next best thing to not having to pay it in the first place.

Let's look at an example. Say we have a money contract balance of $500,000, and the accompanying life insurance policy has a net death benefit of $800,000. At our death, the estate gets $300,000 *more* than the balance in the money contract account. That $300,000 is likely as much - or more than the cumulative cost of all the insurance charges over the years - meaning those lifetime costs are essentially refunded to our estate.

"Who cares - I'm dead," you may ask? You should care - for two reasons. First, leaving a financial legacy is something we should all aspire. Second, for those who do believe in leaving a financial legacy - whether to family, charities, or both - the refund of fees and commissions means you can spend 100% of what you have during your lifetime - and still leave that legacy.

Think about that for a minute. If Jack - a mainstreamer - has $500,000, and wants to leave $100,000 to his children, he only has $400,000 to spend during his lifetime. Jill on the other hand - with the same $500,000 in a money contract - plus a life insurance policy - can live it up on the entire $500,000, knowing that if her net death benefit is $800,000 - she'll leave behind not $100,000, but $300,000 - that's more for her *and* more for her heirs.

Let your mind wander back into the mainstream world for a minute. Imagine going back to your broker or financial advisor and saying,

> *"Tell you what - you can rip me off for all those*
> *exorbitant fees and commissions I just learned about*
> *for the rest of my investing life. All I ask is that when*
> *I'm gone - you refund them - with interest - back to my*
> *estate. Deal?"*

I can save you the time - no deal.

And now you see another reason I am so focused on defense - on eliminating the impact of losses and taxes - and neutralizing the impact of fees and commissions - because you can - it's just a matter of deciding to do so and finding a plan that will honor that goal.

Now before we leave the subject of the "costs" associated with the plan we're starting to see come together, it is important to really drill down what we get for the fees, because they are tangible, measurable, and valuable. The fees and commissions charged in the mainstream world are nebulous, vague, and we rarely know whether we really received any real value for them or not (we've all seen monkeys throw darts at a newspaper stock listing and outperform seasoned investment advisors).

For starters, let's go back to the very beginning. Remember the three failure traps - the only three ways we could fail to secure our (and our family's) financial future? Failure trap Three was, *"Die Before the Job is Done."* We said at the time that we could easily plug this hole with life insurance. In fact, it's the only way to ensure that the job of securing our family's financial future is completed even if we're not here to do it ourselves. We also said it is cheap, readily available, and that if we're responsible people, we simply have to have some.

Well, since it comes with our plan - we have fulfilled that need as part of the plan itself. Any - and I mean ANY alternative mainstream wealth-building route you may choose will require that you purchase life insurance anyway. In those plans, the cost may not be integral to the plan, but it is a cost that must be borne nonetheless. In our plan, it comes with the territory - like getting a free set of Ginsu knives with your purchase.

But our life insurance component does more than just eliminate failure trap number three. And it does more than give us the ability to 1) eliminate risk from our wealth-building journey, 2) exempt us from income taxes forever, and 3) ensure that all fees and commissions are refunded to our estate.

Most life insurance policies (and all that I would ever recommend to a client) offer three additional living benefits. These fall under a rider or endorsement called Accelerated Death Benefits. These riders are most often free - in other words - there is not an additional premium required by the insurance company offering them.

1. Terminal Illness - most policies will allow the policy owner to obtain up to 80% of the net death benefit in the event of a diagnosis of a terminal illness. Since many terminal illnesses are expensive and drawn out, this can provide financial relief to a family that is invaluable at a time of great need. Each policy will vary on what is considered "terminal." Most often, a terminal illness benefit is available when life expectancy is determined to be one year or less, but sometimes it applies when life expectancy is up to two years.
2. Chronic Illness - most policies allow a benefit in the event of a diagnosis of chronic illness. A chronic illness is one that creates a permanent impairment that is not necessarily terminal. Examples include stroke victims, accident victims who sustain paralysis or other physically limiting injuries, or those with cognitive impairments like Alzheimer's, for example.
3. Long-Term-Care - nearly half of us will require long-term-care of one kind or another. In the past, this was often called "nursing

home" care - but today's alternatives are much more broad and palatable. They include in-home care, assisted living, and others. Policies with this feature generally allow a drawdown of 2% of the death benefit per month in the event of a long-term-care need (limitations apply). So a person with a $500,000 death benefit could draw up to $10,000 per month (2% of $500k) for long-term care.

The Chronic and Long-Term-Care benefits typically require 1) a medical diagnosis, and 2) the inability to perform two of the six "activities of daily living" (ADL's). These include:

- Personal hygiene and grooming
- Dressing and undressing
- Self feeding
- Functional transfers (getting into and out of bed or wheelchair, getting onto or off of a toilet, etc.)
- Bowel and bladder management
- Ambulation (walking with or without use of an assistive device [walker, cane, or crutches] or use of a wheelchair)

It's also worth noting that these "accelerated" benefits are most often known as "indemnity" benefits rather than "reimbursement" benefits. In other words, most traditional policies that cover long-term-care costs only reimburse the actual out-of-pocket costs of services. Sometimes, the benefits are even more restrictive, and reimburse "in-patient" care only - like a nursing home or hospital. And the term "reimbursement" often means the costs have to be advanced by the patient or a relative, who must then apply for reimbursement - an inconvenience at best - an impossibility at worst.

An indemnity benefit on the other hand, does not limit the type of service or care. In fact, it doesn't require the owner to procure any service at all. In theory, a person could be incapable of performing two of the six activities of daily living (medically disabled), qualify for the benefit, and use the money to travel the world - buy a house - or do something else completely non-care related.

Now that may seem a bit unrealistic - but what is realistic is that a person falling into this category might prefer in-home care, or care delivered by a relative whom they wish to compensate for doing so.

Only an indemnity-type benefit will allow the policy owner to use absolute discretion regarding the use of the benefit money.

Not only is a traditional long-term-care insurance policy much more restrictive in terms of the kinds of care it will reimburse, it is becoming prohibitively expensive, and, like other kinds of insurance, is a "use-it-or-lose-it" proposition. Because these accelerated benefit riders come without an additional premium charge, they can be invaluable - particularly to those who can't obtain long-term-care coverage.

By the way - since a life insurance death benefit is paid income-tax free - and the benefit we're talking about is an "accelerated" death benefit - it also is paid tax-free in most cases. And the "benefit" - is never accessed as an accelerated benefit, the entire death benefit will go to our heirs - so the accelerated benefit is never a "use-it-or-lose-it" proposition - it's a "get it this way - or get it that way" benefit.

You may be asking yourself - how could someone qualify for life insurance, but not long-term-care insurance? Good question - but it happens more regularly than you might think. For example, many people have a physical condition that could evolve into a need for long-term care - but is completely non-life-threatening. Birth defects and injuries are good examples.

A life insurance policy is offered and priced on the basis of the insurance company's assessment when they will need to pay a death claim. Long-term-care policies are offered and priced on the insurance company's assessment of whether and when a long-term-care benefit claim might need to be paid. Therefore, a person with a non-life-threatening condition that could evolve into a long term care need might not qualify for long-term-care insurance, but might well qualify for life insurance.

Perhaps that was more information than you wanted, but is extremely important to know. It's important because all the costs associated with the plan we've outlined are insurance costs; and they deliver benefits of tangible, measureable value that reach far beyond the traditional death benefit.

Rigged

Chapter 22

Risk-Free, Tax-Free, and Fee Neutral

All in One Package

Here's the big payoff - the "Super-Roth" I alluded to earlier. We've talked about money contracts as a great way to get safety for our money and ensure that we never take a step backward (a loss of principal) like everyone else will inevitably do. Inside our money contract, we talked about being able to grow our money at a fixed rate that would outperform almost any other fixed rate investment we might consider. We also agreed that equity indexing was a way to keep risk out of the equation while giving ourselves much of the market's upside potential - perhaps even out-performing the market itself over an extended term.

In the last chapter, we talked about adding a life insurance component to our plan as a way of neutralizing the impact of fees, knowing that the death benefit will refund whatever fees we may have paid along the way - and then some.

In the middle, we discussed the fact that the issuer of our brand of money contract would also act as a lender who will lend against our money contract account so that we don't have to take money out of our account and pay taxes on it. That's how we achieve the tax-free component.

Now that may seem like a lot of moving parts and be a little overwhelming to some. There's a money contract provider, a lender, and a life insurance company. How can we keep track of all those entities, and how much time and effort will it take to do so?

Here's the great news: all three are included in one single product from one single provider. That single provider is a life insurance company - and that single product is called an Indexed Universal Life Insurance Policy. You may have guessed by now that that was the direction I was headed. But had I told you on page one that life insurance was an excellent way to build wealth, you may never have read past page one.

Most people's paradigm - the things they believe - even if they don't know where those beliefs came from, prohibit them from looking at life insurance objectively. Then there are the so-called gurus of personal finance out there trashing certain types of life insurance - gurus like Dave Ramsey, Suze Orman, Clark Howard and others. To be frank - they are simply mis-informed and have an agenda.

I know life insurance can seem intimidating and confusing – so can the internal combustion engine - but without it, we couldn't get to the grocery store. And I don't intend to use these pages to make you a life insurance expert. What I will suggest however, is that the word "universal" in universal life insurance means that the contract can be constructed in a nearly endless combination of options - kind of like picking out a car and choosing the options, colors, and power plants as you go.

You don't need to become an expert - but you do need to work with a life insurance professional that is. Not one who's a generalist in life insurance, but one who is an expert on designing a universal life platform for maximum wealth building purposes.

Most insurance agents are trained to maximize the amount of death benefit their client gets for the least number of dollars. When it comes to wealth building with life insurance, you need a professional who takes the exact opposite approach - and can get you the most cash buildup possible, for the least amount of insurance (cost) possible.

Here's why. If a properly designed universal life insurance policy could really deliver tax-free, risk-free wealth accumulation plus income - why would anyone invest a penny into anything else? The only reason would be if they thought they could consistently earn a high enough rate of return to outpace the growth of indexed life insurance - *after* accounting for the ravages of investment risk, taxes, and fees and commissions. In other words - few would ever invest a nickel in mainstream vehicles and strategies. Instead - money would pour into life insurance products by the truckload - and that wouldn't make Wall Street very happy.

More importantly, the government wouldn't be very happy - they generate huge tax dollars from the wealth people accumulate, the income they draw from their wealth, and the estate taxes they impose on what's left to others - and I mean huge tax dollars. And we know the government won't allow too much of a good thing. We see it with qualified plans like IRAs, 401(k)s, and Roths. Those plans aren't so good in my opinion - but the government limits the amount of money we can stuff away in them anyway.

Well - the same thing applies to life insurance, but in a little different fashion that actually works in our favor. Rather than putting a hard ceiling on contributions (as they do with qualified plans), they require instead that we purchase a certain amount of life insurance for every dollar we want to put into the money contract account.

That's right - the limiting factor that determines how much we can stuff into a life insurance policy is the amount of death benefit we have to buy along with it! In other words - there is virtually no limit on the amount of money we can put into it - which means there is virtually no limit to the amount of tax-free, risk-free, fee neutral wealth we can build inside an equity-indexed universal life policy.

Now if you just tilted your head to the side and squinted with that puzzled look - you're catching on. Life insurance is a good thing. We know we're buying tomorrow dollars (the death benefit) for pennies today - or less. That's a good thing. And we just spent an entire chapter detailing the other benefits we get from the life insurance account - a bucket of money for long-term-care, for example. We also know that the very presence of the life insurance account gives us the ability to borrow from the insurance company on a tax-free and penalty-free basis.

But the government-imposed insurance minimums are positioned as if they're a penalty - or disincentive of some kind. Isn't that like Mom telling us that to get one scoop of ice cream after dinner, we'll have to eat two cinnamon rolls first? (my weakness - cinnamon rolls). Sure there's a cost for every dollar of pure life insurance we have to put in our life insurance account, but we also get *value* for each of those dollars.

The minimum amount of pure life insurance required in a universal life insurance policy is defined by three pieces of federal legislation that have evolved over the years, known as DEFRA, TEFRA, and TAMRA. It's not important to know what these are and how they work - but it is supremely important that your insurance company and your universal life insurance professional know how they work.

In most cases, these requirements will force enough life insurance into an insurance-based wealth building plan to accomplish everything we need in terms of death benefit protection, so most insurance professionals will help you design your plan with the minimum amount of life insurance for the amount you want to save. That way the maximum dollars are going into the money contract, and the fewest dollars are going into the "cost of insurance" - while keeping the policy in total compliance with DEFRA, TEFRA, and TAMRA.

But if those minimums are not adequate for your pure insurance need, you can always put more pure insurance into the insurance account. A true professional will help you comply with the minimums, ensure that you have the right amount of insurance you need for your family - and do it all in a way that *maximizes* wealth accumulation at the *lowest* possible cost.

Now because the life insurance component costs money - and that cost is higher for older folks than it is for the young, does that mean universal life insurance is a wealth building platform for only the young?

Not at all. While it's true that a dollar of life insurance benefit costs more for a 70 year old than it does for a 20 year old, our old friends DEFRA, TEFRA, and TAMRA do us another favor. The older we get, the less pure insurance they require us to buy. So while the cost of that insurance goes up per $1,000 of death benefit - the amount we have to buy goes down as roughly depicted in the chart below. The net result is that our strategy will perform almost as well for a 60 year-old as it will a 30-year old.

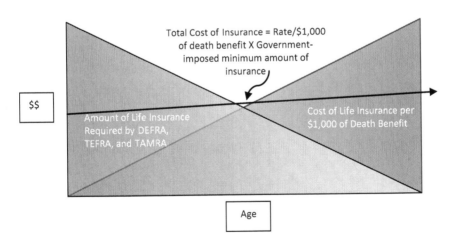

Since our "need" for life insurance generally goes down as we age anyway - this too is usually a positive rather than a negative. The more wealth we've accumulated, the less the risk of premature death - so the less pure insurance we need. The net effect of all this is that using universal life insurance as a wealth building platform is just as effective for older folks as it is for younger folks.

Because life insurance doesn't have a hard contribution ceiling like qualified plans, it means there is no government-imposed limit on the amount of money we can put into a wealth building life insurance platform. So whether you're committed to saving a few hundred dollars a month, or a few hundred thousand a month, you can do so with life insurance. The only "limit" will be the insurance company's "appetite" for providing you pure life insurance - but that is a limit few will ever approach.

Rigged

Chapter 23

Plan "B"

Okay - that makes sense - but in all this talk about life insurance, one thing we've ignored so far is that not everyone can qualify for life insurance. Remember, life insurance is an "underwritten" product - meaning you can't just go pluck a policy off the shelf. It is a contract - and as we discussed earlier - it has to be offered and accepted. Life insurance companies are pretty good about not offering life insurance to those with life expectancies that don't meet certain criteria - in particular - those with serious health issues. So - is there a wealth building option that fits our criteria - our rule-set - for people who are either completely uninsurable - or for those for whom the cost of the insurance would be prohibitive?

The answer is...mostly...yes - and coincidently - it comes from the same source - an insurance company. Insurance companies sell only two kinds of products - life insurance and annuities. So Plan "B" - is an annuity. Now without getting deep into the weeds, let's take a quick look at what an annuity is, how it works, and why it fulfills *most* of our wealth building criteria.

The easy way to think of annuities is to compare them to an old-fashioned pension plan - the kind your parents might have had - the kind people liked - and the kind that have all but disappeared today.

In a pension plan, an employer contributes a set portion of our salary to the plan. In retirement, the pension plan pays a monthly benefit until death (some even have features that extend payments through the life of a surviving spouse). An annuity is a private pension plan. We set aside a bit of money, and the insurance company guarantees a lifetime income, or an income that can be designed to continue through the life of a surviving spouse - just like a traditional pension.

Where the two differ is in the amount of retirement income we'll receive. In a traditional pension, the guaranteed retirement income is usually tied to our working wage. In an annuity, because it is a personal, rather than group plan, our guaranteed lifetime income is a function of our contributions plus whatever growth the insurance company has guaranteed us - or credited to our account over the years.

While today's annuities can make themselves quite complicated, understand that - at their core, an annuity has three components.

- Premium Contributions - what you put into them - either in lump sum, or periodic contributions over time
- Accumulation - what growth the insurance company guarantees - either by amount (as in a certain guaranteed percentage of annual growth), or by definition (the stock market subject to a floor and a cap [as in equity-indexing])
- Distributions - the lifetime guaranteed income the insurance company will pay based on the accumulated value of the annuity account (one form of distribution is a death benefit, which many annuities include as an added feature).

Because the most recent generation is largely unfamiliar with traditional company-sponsored pensions, the most common modern day example of an annuity is Social Security. A portion of our income is paid into the social security trust fund over time, and a guaranteed stream of income payments is made from retirement until death. We may quarrel about how good a job the government does with our money – but we never turn down the check. In fact, we are awfully glad it's there when the time comes.

Annuities - as a category - are highly popular because they're the *only product in existence* that comes with a contractually guaranteed lifetime income. As such, they offer the security of a fixed monthly income, and - perhaps more importantly - the assurance that no matter how long we live, we'll never outlive our income.

That last concept is an extremely important one to fully understand. We'll explore it in a minute. But one question that typically comes to mind at this point is how a company can guarantee a lifetime income. It's easier to see how a government can do it - but less obvious how a company can do it. And even if a company can - why an insurance company? Why is an insurance company the only place that offers an annuity - a private pension plan?

Skip this if you wish – it's not critical to our discussion, but I think it's interesting. If you understand how Vegas makes book (takes bets), then you understand how an insurance company works. Let's say the Colts are playing the Patriots this weekend. Vegas has set the "line" at Colts -3. That means the Colts are giving up three points, and must win by 4 or more for a person betting on the Colts, to win the bet. Even if the Colts win – but by just 2 points, a person taking the Colts loses the bet because of the point spread.

Many people mistakenly believe that football odds-makers are experts who base the point spread on their incredible football prowess. The truth is, the odds makers are completely disinterested in who wins and who loses or by how much.

The line exists for the sole purpose of attracting a roughly equal number of dollars to each side of a bet. In the example above, by setting the line at Colts -3, they've found that they'll attract an equal number of dollars betting **on** the Colts (where betters are giving up three points), as will come in **against** the Colts (for the Patriots since betters are getting a three point advantage).

Why do they structure it this way? Because they don't take outcome-based risks. They understand that rule number one is, First, Lose No Money. They take a small percentage of the total book (dollars bet), using the losers' money to pay off the winners. In that regard, the only way they can "lose" anything is if there is more wagered on one side of the line versus the other. When wagers are balanced, they are "outcome agnostic."

Do bets become unbalanced? Of course – which is why lines "move" right up to game time. When too much money is coming in on one side of the bet, the odds makers "move" the line to create an incentive for more money to be bet on the opposing side, thus balancing the bets and eliminating any outcome-based risk.

Insurance companies work in much the same way. The "outcome" that is the source of all insurance company risk is life expectancy. As we already noted, insurance companies sell two kinds of products. Life insurance is the insurance company's bet that you're going to live a long time. That's why life insurance is offered only to the healthy (or to the slightly unhealthy - but at a higher cost). While that may sound counter-intuitive, think of it this way. How does a life insurance company maximize its profits on life insurance? They acquire premium-paying *policyholders who live long lives and pay premiums for a long time. More revenue - and a longer time delay until a death claim has to be paid means more profit. They lose when the policyholder steps into a busy intersection the day after paying his first premium.*

In similar fashion, an annuity is "anti-life-insurance" because it is a "bet" that the policyholder is not going to live to their life expectancy. An annuity is also funded through premium payments. Those premiums are invested, and the "annuitant" is guaranteed an income stream for life. But what if we buy an annuity one day, and take an unfortunate step into a busy intersection the next? The insurance company keeps all the deposits we've made, plus all the earnings on those deposits, less any annuity payments made to us. In other words, they win when we live shorter than our life expectancy, and lose if we live longer – exactly the opposite of life insurance.

Now not every annuity contract lets the insurance company keep the remaining balance, but one of the key reasons life insurance companies sell life insurance and annuities – and nothing else – is that they are perfect "risk" offsets to one another. Just as the Vegas bookie wants an equal number of dollars for an outcome and against an outcome, so does an insurance company.

They accomplish that by offering two products that straddle opposite sides of the same life expectancy variable. Those products are labeled Life Insurance - and Annuities.

So how does an annuity serve as a Plan "B" wealth building strategy? Because it meets most of our criteria. For example, we can put an unlimited amount of funding into an annuity.

Like life insurance, earnings can be credited in one of three ways – fixed, variable, or equity-indexed. You'll recall the definitions of each from the life insurance section. Remember, we will not discuss variable annuities here since they don't satisfy our "lose no money" rule. Instead, we'll focus our attention on the fixed and equity-indexed options.

Three characteristics set annuities apart from all other investment vehicles, and it's important we understand each:

<u>Tax-Deferral</u> – The next best thing to paying no taxes, is deferring the payment of taxes into the future. Earnings on deferred annuities are not taxed until taken out, making them very efficient tax planning instruments.

While we can achieve tax deferral on all sorts of qualified plans (401(k)s, IRAs and the like), the advantage annuities have over those alternatives is that when they're funded with after-tax dollars (taxes have already been paid on the contribution portion of our annuity balance - and presumably at yesterday's cheaper tax rates - a portion of the income payments coming from the annuity is considered a return of already-taxed principal. The rest is considered investment income. The return of principal portion is not taxed at all, while the "growth" portion is taxed at current income tax rates.

The insurance company will do the math, and report to you what portion is a return of principal (the "exclusion ratio") and which is taxable earnings. They do this by issuing a 1099.

One note about lifetime income. In discussing the tax-deferral feature above, we mentioned that annuity income comes with an exclusion ratio – a portion of the payment that is considered a return of principal and therefore is not taxed. The return of principal portion is determined by dividing all deposits by the annuitant's life expectancy. So let's say an annuitant had deposited $100,000 into their annuity. At the point of annuitization, if life expectancy were 10 years, then $10,000 of each annual payment would be a return of principal and included in the exclusion ratio (excluded from taxation). After ten years however, all payments would be considered earnings, and therefore fully taxable.

Annuities can also be purchased inside qualified plans like IRAs. Since the tax-deferral benefit is inherent in the IRA in the first place, there is no additional tax benefit to an annuity inside a qualified plan. Whether an annuity is owned outside a tax-qualified plan, or inside one, they offer two substantial benefits over just about any other investment:

135

Lifetime Income Guarantee – Even if the balance in the annuity account has been completely exhausted through income payments, the insurance company guarantees that income will continue for life. No other instrument can offer such a guarantee.

No Risk to Principal – Fixed and indexed growth options protect principal and lock in earnings 100%, which is fundamental to our rule set.

In general, the trade-off for a lifetime income guarantee is that the insurance company keeps any undistributed balance when an annuitant dies prior to their life expectancy. In other words, it is possible that an annuity could be funded with $100,000 today, make one payment to the annuitant of $1,000 - who then dies - and the insurance company keeps the remaining $99,000 for themselves. Because this is a concern to many, most "modern" annuity products provide at least a partial death benefit feature to alleviate this potential outcome.

Just a few more words about the value of guaranteed lifetime income. You'll recall that our rule number one was, "Failure is not an option." You may also recall that failure trap 3 was, "dying before we've secured our family's financial future." Life insurance is a critical piece of our financial plan no matter how boring, complicated, distasteful or morbid the subject may be. It is the only way of mitigating our *mortality* risk – the risk that we die before our financial goals are fully funded. Our Mortality risk is highest when we have a young family, a mortgage, a car payment, and when college, weddings, retirement and grandkids lay ahead.

But if life goes as planned, we build wealth, reduce debt, and move past some of those costly life events. As this happens, our mortality risk goes down - and that's a good thing. If the kids are through college, the house is paid off, and we have money in the bank, the financial fallout from our premature death – as emotionally tragic as it might be – is reduced.

But just as our mortality fades into the rearview mirror, another life risk begins to intensify – our longevity risk. Longevity risk is the risk that we live too long rather than too short – and outlive the savings we've accumulated.

Fifty years ago, life expectancy wasn't even 70. Today, life expectancy is closing in on 80 years – with women adding about a month of life expectancy each year. According to USA Today:

> "... In fact, there's a 41% chance that a 62-year-old woman today will live to 90; a 62-year-old man has a 29% chance. For a married couple, there's a 58% chance that one of them will live to 90 and a 29% chance that one will reach 95."

The point is, as we age, we evolve from high mortality risk to high longevity risk. The chart below shows the relationship between mortality risk (the risk of dying prematurely) and longevity risk (the risk of outliving our financial assets).

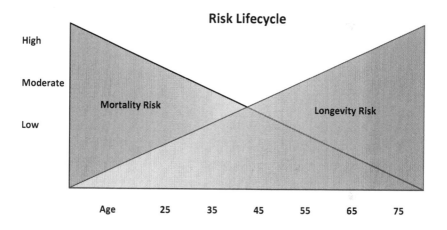

Say you did it all right – you saved, you invested wisely, you didn't make too many mistakes, and now it's time to stop working for money and let your money work for you. You're 70, you've accumulated $1,000,000 in savings, and it's time to retire. Here's the $64,000 question:

How much can you begin spending each year and still have the certainty that you'll never run out?

The question is unanswerable unless your crystal ball can tell you exactly when you'll receive your "final promotion." And even if you knew exactly how long your money needed to last, you still wouldn't be able to factor in the unexpected – things like big medical expenses and the like. Without those answers, too many people live in fear of running out of money, and resign themselves to a lifestyle that's far below what they envisioned while they were saving.

I find that tragic. And it's why annuities are so important. Guaranteed lifetime income cannot, by definition, be outlived. In that sense, we should think of annuities as longevity insurance – which is just as critical as life insurance was in an earlier phase of life.

Both mortality and longevity risks are always with us, but they intensify at an inverse rate. The graph above attempts to show that as mortality risk diminishes, longevity risk intensifies – but neither disappear altogether.

Now you know more about annuities than many of the people selling them. In fact, you may know more than you ever wanted to know. But there's a reason this was important. If you can't qualify for life insurance and build wealth the way we outlined previously - or if the cost of insurance due to health or age is prohibitive, then annuities might just be your best Plan "B" solution.

They fit most of the components of our rule set. Our money is immunized from market risk. Income from an annuity is tax-deferred and partially tax-free as it comes out. Fees and commissions are reasonable. And some annuities have features like guaranteed death benefits, long-term-care riders, and others. Their biggest benefit is that their income payout is guaranteed for life.

While I clearly believe equity-indexed life insurance is the most powerful wealth building vehicle in existence - and likely to get even better as traditional markets remain volatile and taxes continue their steady ascent upward - annuities fit the bill in three specific situations:

1. When access to life insurance is either impossible or cost prohibitive,
2. When there is not much time between the accumulation phase and the distribution phase (life insurance works best when funded for a minimum of 5 years before starting income), or
3. When the guarantee of inexhaustible lifetime income trumps the need for tax-free income.

Chapter 24

Plan "A" for Business Owners
and the Self - Employed

When it comes to building wealth as a self-employed business owner, the landscape is tricky. No one knows better the ravages of taxes than the business owner - so tax-qualified plans like the 401(k), the SEP, the SIMPLE, the Keogh, and others - can be alluringly attractive.

While each of these different variations of tax-qualified plans have their nuanced differences, their fundamental mechanics are the same. They all allow a limited number of pre-tax dollars to be set aside for saving and investing.

The set-aside money grows on a tax-deferred basis, meaning more dollars stay inside the plan to compound, so there is potential for more dollars to end up in the plan account. Taxes are then paid when money is taken out - and that may be a long way down the road.

Despite their attractiveness, there are several reasons business owners and the self-employed would rather not use a qualified plan - and all are very important:

- Contribution Limits - All qualified plans limit how much money can be socked away, and often those limits are well below what the business owner may like to put into a wealth-building plan.
- Use-it-or-Lose-it Contributions - Business owners know that in some years, there may not be enough profit to fully fund their own qualified account. Perhaps it's not even a question of profits - perhaps an expansion or acquisition opportunity that consumed the cash that they would otherwise contribute. Cruelly, there are no "carry-forward" minutes in qualified plans - you can't use the unused contribution capacity next year. If it's not used - it's gone forever.
- Non-Discrimination Rules - For those business owners with employees, non-discrimination rules require that qualified plans must be offered to most employees. They can also require that if company-wide participation is disproportionate (too many

high-earning employees participating - and not enough lower-earning employees participating) plan contributions can be *dis*qualified. Not only can this further limit the business owner's ability to fund these plans, offering them broadly gets to be very expensive.

- Liquidity - getting access to money that's already been contributed to a qualified plan comes with a quadruple tax whammy.

To demonstrate the quadruple tax whammy, let's consider Mark, who owns a sign company. He's built up a nice tax-qualified account through the business, and has an opportunity to buy a struggling competitor for $100,000. It's a great opportunity to build market share, acquire some new assets, and get a couple of people that can help him grow his business. But a conversation with his tax accountant reveals the true price of funding the acquisition using his qualified money.

- **Whammy No. 1** - Mark will be taxed on every dollar he withdraws (since none of it has yet been taxed).

- **Whammy No. 2** - Mark cannot take advantage of capital gains tax rates - his withdrawal will be taxed as ordinary income no matter how long he has held the underlying investment.

- **Whammy No. 3** - Mark will have to pay a 10% penalty on his withdrawal since he's under age 59-1/2.

- **Whammy No. 4** - Mark and Dierdra (his wife) will pay a higher tax rate on their regular annual income, because the withdrawal is added to that income, which thrusts them into a higher tax bracket.

Let's play out the scenario to see just how devastating the liquidity penalties of tax-qualified plans can be to business owners.

Mark needs $100,000 to take advantage of the opportunity. He has over $400,000 in his account - so it's a logical source of money to complete the transaction. He goes to his accountant to run the idea by him. The accountant first points out that Mark and Dierdra's regular "earned" income (combined) of $100,000 puts them in the

25% tax bracket, leaving them with after-tax income of $75,000 - which they need to support their lifestyle. But if they withdraw $100,000 from Mark's qualified plan, it will be added to their regular income - taking their total taxable income to $200,000 that year. At $200,000, the accountant informs them they'll be in the 35% tax bracket.

Mark reminds him that the investments he's going to sell from inside his qualified plan have been held for more than one year - so they should only be taxed at the lower capital gain tax rate. Unfortunately, the accountant corrects him - 100% of qualified funds are taxed as ordinary income under all circumstances. Capital gain rates never apply to qualified funds.

Then of course, there's the 10% penalty for early withdrawal from a qualified plan; and by now, Mark is doing the double take with his accountant - the same guy who suggested setting up the qualified plan in the first place.

Mark does the math. How much will he need to take out of his tax-qualified plan in order to end up with $100,000 for the acquisition - and without reducing the couple's $75,000 after-tax living income?

The answer: a whopping $200,000.

When Mark takes $200,000 out of his qualified plan - he'll pay 35% in income taxes, plus the 10% early withdrawal penalty. That's a total of 45%, which will leave him with $110,000 - exactly enough to make the $100,000 acquisition and reimburse he and Deidra for the extra $10,000 of personal income taxes they'll pay on their regular income resulting from the higher tax bracket that year.

Their liquidity penalty: An effective tax rate of 50% and a total "liquidity cost" of $100,000.

Even without the quadruple whammy of the liquidity penalty, business owners, entrepreneurs and self-employed professionals are left with an important question. Should I establish and contribute to a qualified plan - or not? Let's take a side-by-side look at two different scenarios.

Jack and Jill are small business owners. They both commit to saving and investing $5,000/year starting at age 30, and keeping it up until they retire at 70. Jack puts his money into a tax-qualified plan because he's attracted to bright shiny objects with names like pre-tax contributions, tax-deferred growth, and the prospect of lower tax rates in retirement.

Jill on the other hand, understands the liquidity penalty - and decides to bite the bullet, pay taxes on the money she socks away - and retain constant, penalty-free access (liquidity) to her money in the event of an emergency or opportunity. Even though she deposits less each year ($4,000 vs. Jack's $5,000) because her income is taxed at 20%, she's confident that her outcome will be better than Jack's.

Jack's Qualified Plan | Jill's Non-Qualified Plan

Age	Beg Bal	Deposit	End Bal	Beg Bal	Deposit	End Bal
30	-	5,000	5,360	-	4,000	4,288
31	5,360	5,000	11,106	4,288	4,000	8,885
32	11,106	5,000	17,266	8,885	4,000	13,812
33	17,266	5,000	23,869	13,812	4,000	19,095
34	23,869	5,000	30,947	19,095	4,000	24,758
35	30,947	5,000	38,535	24,758	4,000	30,828
36	38,535	5,000	46,670	30,828	4,000	37,336
37	46,670	5,000	55,390	37,336	4,000	44,312
38	55,390	5,000	64,738	44,312	4,000	51,791
39	64,738	5,000	74,759	51,791	4,000	59,808
40	74,759	5,000	85,502	59,808	4,000	68,402
41	85,502	5,000	97,018	68,402	4,000	77,615
42	97,018	5,000	109,364	77,615	4,000	87,491
43	109,364	5,000	122,598	87,491	4,000	98,078
44	122,598	5,000	136,785	98,078	4,000	109,428
45	136,785	5,000	151,993	109,428	4,000	121,595
46	151,993	5,000	168,297	121,595	4,000	134,637
47	168,297	5,000	185,774	134,637	4,000	148,619
48	185,774	5,000	204,510	148,619	4,000	163,608
49	204,510	5,000	224,595	163,608	4,000	179,676
50	224,595	5,000	246,125	179,676	4,000	196,900
51	246,125	5,000	269,207	196,900	4,000	215,365
52	269,207	5,000	293,949	215,365	4,000	235,160
53	293,949	5,000	320,474	235,160	4,000	256,379

54	320,474	5,000	348,908	256,379	4,000	279,126
55	348,908	5,000	379,389	279,126	4,000	303,511
56	379,389	5,000	412,065	303,511	4,000	329,652
57	412,065	5,000	447,094	329,652	4,000	357,675
58	447,094	5,000	484,645	357,675	4,000	387,716
59	484,645	5,000	524,899	387,716	4,000	419,919
60	524,899	5,000	568,052	419,919	4,000	454,441
61	568,052	5,000	614,312	454,441	4,000	491,449
62	614,312	5,000	663,902	491,449	4,000	531,122
63	663,902	5,000	717,063	531,122	4,000	573,650
64	717,063	5,000	774,052	573,650	4,000	619,241
65	774,052	5,000	835,143	619,241	4,000	668,115
66	835,143	5,000	900,634	668,115	4,000	720,507
67	900,634	5,000	970,839	720,507	4,000	776,671
68	970,839	5,000	1,046,100	776,671	4,000	836,880
69	1,046,100	5,000	**1,126,779**	836,880	4,000	**901,423**

Both grow their money at the exact same rate - in this case - 7.2% per year. When we fast-forward to their respective retirements, we find that Jack has built a qualified account valued at $1,126,779. He's quite proud of his accomplishment.

Jill - on the other hand, used the kind of Plan A approach we described in an earlier chapter - an Equity-Indexed Life Insurance Policy. Her tax rate during the accumulation years was 20% thanks to home mortgage interest deductions, exemptions for kids, and other credits and deductions. That meant that of the $5,000/year she committed to saving, just $4,000 made its way into her account - the rest was paid in taxes along the way.

At her pre-retirement consult - she learned that she has $901,423 - not nearly as impressive as Jack's $1.126 million. But her money comes out tax-free - she has no silent partner in her plan, so she owns it all. Jack on the other hand, whose retirement tax rate is 30%, realizes that he only owns $788,745 of that $1.126 million showing on his account statement.

Suddenly, what - on paper - looked like a $225,000 *advantage* for Jack, turns out to be a $113,000 *advantage* for Jill, considering the after-tax implications.

Jill paid $40,000 in taxes along the way - 20% of her contributions over her investing lifetime. Jack deferred the exact same amount, getting the benefit of his full $5,000 going into his investment account. But at the end of the day, that $40,000 was all Jill paid - ever. Jack deferred - and compounded his tax bill so that rather than $40,000, he ballooned it all the way up to $338,033.

And before we leave the subject, Jack and Jill will spend nearly 20 years in retirement. What happens 5 years in, if Congress decides to increase income tax rates? Jack pays the higher rate - further reducing his standard of living, while Jill got off the tax Merry-Go-Round years ago.

The point is - tax-qualified plans are no good for lifetime needs like funding college, buying a house, replacing a car, paying for a wedding, etc., because of the onerous liquidity penalty. They're no good for business needs for the same reason. But the tax, penalty, and liquidity implications of qualified plans are not the only factors for small businesses to consider.

A relatively new phenomenon is employer fiduciary liability - where employees and employee groups are suing employers over the cost of fees and commissions, as well as the performance of qualified plans.

The simple fact is that most qualified plans offer limited investment choices, and trial lawyers - who have run out of cigarette companies to sue - have latched on to these limitations and built lawsuits out of them, holding employers liable for both the poor performance of the "investments" the employer has "chosen" for the employees, as well as the fees charged to plan participants. Not fair - just fact.

In just the last few years, lawsuits have prevailed against such giants as Wal-Mart, Ameriprise, Caterpillar, General Dynamics, and others (see the Reuters article at reuters.com/article/2011/10/04/us-retirement-fundlawsuit-idUSTRE7935DH20111004).

Against the backdrop of the other limitations we discussed earlier (contribution limits, liquidity constraints, use-it-or-lose-it provisions, non-discrimination issues, etc.), qualified plans offer just two *ad*vantages: pre-tax contributions and tax-deferred growth - both of which, as our analysis shows, are red herrings.

Here's my alternative - at least for the business owner and key employees. Use an equity-indexed universal life insurance policy as a savings vehicle for yourself and your key employees.

Let's see how that might work out.

You had a good year - and you have $50,000 of profit that, because your business is organized as a pass-thru, is going to be taxed as ordinary income to you. The tax bill on that profit is estimated at $15,000 - even though it won't be "due" until April. The solution: deposit $50,000 into an Equity-indexed Universal Life policy. When the tax bill comes due in April, ask the insurance company for a $15,000 advance on the life insurance benefit, and pay your taxes with the insurance company's money. That way, your $50,000 (minus the costs of insurance) is growing on an equity-indexed basis (with the stock market, subject to a floor and a cap), and you've used the insurance company's money to pay the tax - never to face a nickel of tax on that money again.

Like shampooing - when next year comes - rinse/lather/repeat. Next year may be better - or not quite as good. The cash in your policy is likely to have enough earnings to pay the cost of insurance into the future even if you don't make another deposit for a year or two.

Now - if you're like our friend Mark - and a few years down the road you have $400,000 in your policy and a chance to buy a competitor for $100,000, you can get the money out of your insurance policy - no tax, no penalty - so long as adequate borrowing capacity remains - which it will if the policy is managed properly.

Two final points. First, don't get hung up on $50,000 - or a one-time deposit of any amount. If it's easier for you to put in $500/month, the same general math applies.

Second, you can do this for key employees in lieu of a bonus. If you were going to bonus an employee $10,000 - you could give them the cash - and after taxes, they'd have around $7,000. Or - you could deposit $10,000 into an equity-indexed life policy. The employee would then have the option of taking an advance on the life insurance benefit to pay the $3,000 tax liability - and still have their $10,000 of bonus money (less the cost of the insurance) in their money contract account - growing - compounding - accumulating - tax-free and risk-free - not to mention the other benefits we've touched on like the life insurance benefit and the long-term-care type benefit.

Rigged

Chapter 25

Plan "A" for the Wage Earning Employee

Those who are fortunate enough to take home a paycheck benefit from a number of financial advantages, most of which make day-to-day life a little easier to navigate. When the bills come monthly, it's nice to know the income does too. Wage-earning employees used to have another distinct advantage - the company pension plan. Traditional pension plans typically paid a portion of one's working salary in retirement - for life. But those plans saddled the employer with a great deal of risk.

- They bore the risk of funding them adequately to meet the future obligations they made to their employees.

- They bore the risk of investing those funds successfully enough to build a war-chest of money from which lifetime pension benefits could be paid.

- They bore the longevity risk of paying benefits to retirees who may have significantly outlived their life expectancy.

The employee bore little or no risk. They simply retired and collected that monthly check for the rest of their lives - or perhaps a slightly reduced benefit that would be paid for the rest of a spouse's life, too. But because of the cost and risk associated with them - they've largely gone away in the private sector, and their public sector cousins (pensions for teachers, fire-fighters, police, and others) are headline news because of the cost, risk, and underfunded liabilities they have imposed on we - the tax-payers (another good reason to opt out of the taxable realm).

Traditional pensions are called "defined benefit" plans because the retirement benefit is defined - usually as a portion of the employee's working wage. Beginning in the '70s however, it was out with the defined benefit plan - in with the "defined contribution" plan - also known as a 401(k), Keogh, SEP, Simple, and a few others.

Those plans are "sponsored" by employers, but their care and feeding are the responsibility of the employee. They're called defined contribution plans because the only "known" among the variables that define them is what the employee puts into them. The output - or retirement benefit - is unknown, and relies on the saving rate and growth rate those savings may (or may not) benefit from.

Company sponsored defined contribution plans were heralded as a great advance for the employee. For the first time, a wage-earning employee was able to defer income taxes on their wages by directing a portion of their earnings into these tax-deferred plans. For the first time, the employee wasn't "limited" to retirement income that was dictated by the employer. For the first time, an employee could "port" the money they accumulated in one employer-sponsored plan - to another employer-sponsored plan (or roll it into a self-directed IRA) - meaning they didn't have to stay with an employer forever in order to build a retirement benefit.

But these benefits were the whipped cream - they looked tasty - but what lies underneath might not be quite so appetizing upon further inspection. We've already mentioned that these plans allow the employer to shift 100% of the funding, investing, and longevity risk from their books, onto the employee. And we've already learned that the tax-man was able to ensure that as we grew our accounts, we were growing his share of the partnership to its maximum level. Now, we're going to learn about another "underbelly" disadvantage of the tax-qualified plan - it's cost.

As I talk to employee groups, I'm always fascinated at what happens when I ask people what their 401(k) (or similar alternative plan) costs them? Not only will most say it costs them nothing - they'll often argue the point - strenuously.

The discussion gets even more heated when I reveal that in fact - the fees, costs and commissions associated with qualified plans make them the most expensive way to invest there is.

On the off chance that you may be having a similar reaction - let me explain. I'll start with the term "tax-qualified" itself. What does that mean? It means that the plan has to meet certain government criteria in order to "qualify" for the benefits associated with it. More to the point, it means a bunch of legalese that is so complicated and fraught with landmines that can become very costly for the employer - that most hire a "third-party administrator" to take on the burden of establishing the plan document (the structure of the plan), ensuring regulatory compliance, creating and submitting reports, and administering other elements of the plan. The cost of the services of a third party administrator (TPA) is huge - and is passed on to the plan participants.

After those costs, plans bring on an investment firm to define what investment alternatives will be offered, how they'll be offered, when/how/if they'll be changed/updated. They execute trades ordered by perhaps hundreds of plan participants, prepare statements, and maintain a staff to communicate with plan participants on demand.

We're still not done. Not only does the investment advisor/advisory firm get paid by "the plan" (translate: you - the participant), but they typically offer "off-the-shelf" investments like mutual funds, money markets, and others - for which the companies, advisors, and exchanges offering those investments also get paid - by guess who?

Add it all up, and the qualified plan food chain - the layers and layers of "takers" who have to get paid before you do - have made qualified plans the most expensive way to build wealth in existence. And yet - many still argue that the company plan costs them nothing - how can that be?

It can be - because the food-chain has - over time - cleverly figured out ways to bury and disguise costs, fees, and commissions in ways that either don't have to be reported at all, or can be so obscured that you and I can't possibly discern them.

That's why millions can look at their statements and discover a complete disconnect between the relatively good performance of the stock market - and the comparatively anemic performance of their 401(k) statement (check out a recent YouTube video of a 60-Minutes piece on 401(k) fees and commissions at http://www.youtube.com/watch?v=nAHgr9dY9BU).

And in case you think this is overkill, know that the Federal Government is so concerned about the problem, they passed legislation that went into effect in mid-2012, requiring that new fee disclosures accompany qualified plan statements - legislation the investment advisory industry fought tooth and nail.

Successful lawsuits by employees and employer groups related to excessive fees and commissions continue to escalate - and succeed. The simple fact is there could be no lawsuits, judgments, or awards - if first - there were no fees.

So what are the fees in a qualified plan? Consider this from a recent CNN Money article:

> The disclosures will offer 401(k) investors, who collectively control more than $3 trillion, the chance to see what until now has been buried in "additional statements" or 200-page government filings. The simple fact is, many 401(k) plans are much too expensive. The average investor is charged 0.83% of assets annually. (In small plans it's often much more, as high as 3%; in large plans, a little less.) Some plans tack on additional "wrap fees" of up to 1% of your assets. Then there are the mutual funds inside the 401(k)s. Many plans only offer funds that charge fees of 1.5% or more -- far higher than the 0.77% median fee for stock funds. Consider this jarring figure: An ordinary American household with two working adults will cough up almost $155,000 in 401(k) fees over a lifetime, according to the think tank Demos. Says Edward Siedle, a former SEC lawyer who now runs a pension and 401(k) research firm: "401(k)s are leaking money like a sieve."

Add it all up and it's a staggering number, and may help explain why - in an environment where the stock market may be going up by 6-8% - your 401(k) statement seems to be virtually stuck in neutral.

The conclusion we can draw is that company-sponsored tax-qualified plans mix a little tax-deferral, maybe a pinch of company matching funds, a dash of "everybody's doing it," and a dose of "how else am I going to have a decent retirement," and the intoxicating elixir that results numbs us to the reality of the facts:

- The money we put into a company sponsored tax-qualified plan is very expensive to grow as measured by the associated fees and commissions.
- Only about 60-70% of matching contributions (assuming there are any), which are advertised as "free money" from the employer - is ours. The rest belongs to Uncle Sam the minute it shows up in our account.
- The figure that appears on that monthly statement isn't ours - our silent partner owns roughly a third of it in the form of our deferred tax liability.

- Our money is illiquid - and if we need to get at it - we face the quadruple liquidity whammy detailed in the previous chapter.
- Tax-qualified plans are useless for pre-retirement needs like college, weddings, buying a home, or other emergencies and opportunities.
- We'll never know - until the day we start taking money out - how much of it is really ours - because we won't know - until that day - what tax rates will be.

Just to up the ante - let's take what we've learned so far, and consider the diagram below.

Hierarchy of Money

Free Money

Tax-Free Money

Value

Tax-Deferred Money

Taxable Money

What the hierarchy tells us is that to the extent we can control the acquisition and characterization of our money, our first priority needs to be obtaining all the free money we can get first, tax-free money next, tax-deferred money after that, with taxable money making up the rest.

For the wage earner, the money we earn in the form of a wage, salary, commission or bonus - is *taxable* money - the least valuable kind - in terms of our present discussion. But if we can contribute some of that taxable money into the company-sponsored tax-qualified plan - we can instantly convert it into the more valuable *tax-deferred* money category.

That's a good start. It gets even better if the company has a matching program, which triggers the release of some free money into our account. So:

1. We earn taxable money

2. We can convert some of it to the tax-deferred category by contributing to the qualified plan,

3. And in doing so - we might get some free money in the form of company matching funds.

But we've skipped the second most valuable form of money - tax-free money. In a typical scenario, a company might match 50% of our contributions up to, say 5%. So if we choose to be really diligent savers - and defer 10% of our income into the company plan, the company's matching policy would match 50% of our first 5% with free money!

Even though we can feel good about our commitment to saving - voluntarily skipping the tax-free category isn't the smartest way for us to complete the wealth-building task.

Before we get lost in the numbers, let's look at an example:

John's Salary	$60,000
Deferral into the company 401(k)	10% = $6,000
Company Match:	50% of first 5% = $1,500

John would get the same $1,500 of free money if he cut his contribution in half, to 5% of his salary, or $3,000 instead. If John wants to save the full 10%, then he should put the other 5% (or $3,000) into a tax-free vehicle, since tax-free money would be more valuable than putting the whole thing into the tax-deferred 401(k) plan.

What vehicle do we know that builds wealth tax-free? There are three - but two don't meet our "First, Lose No Money" test.

1. The Roth IRA has become a more popular vehicle as tax rates have ramped up over the years. A Roth really isn't an investment - rather an account "shell" that is tax-favored. What goes in the Roth is the real challenge because most any investment we might hold inside them can lose value. They also carry a liquidity risk. Taking money out of a Roth prior to age 59-1/2 still triggers a penalty. Finally, the contribution limits on the

Roth are so severe, they can only - at best - supplement retirement, not provide for it on their own.

2. <u>Tax-Free Bonds</u> - May give us tax-free interest income, but as we've discussed in previous chapters, their susceptibility to principal loss disqualifies them under our "First, Lose No Money" rule.

3. <u>Cash Value Life Insurance</u> - on the other hand has no contribution limits, allows access to our accumulated wealth tax-free - and penalty-free (even pre-retirement), and meets all the other Five Money Needs we talked about earlier.

Here's the bottom line for wage earners. Despite their shortcomings, I always recommend you take all the free money you can get. Unless future tax rates are 100%, taxes will never eat up *all* the free money – so take it. HOWEVER, **stop** contributing tax-deferred money when you've reached the maximum employer match, and instead move the next dollar saved into a tax-free vehicle since tax-free money is more valuable than tax-deferred money.

If you've arrived at the same conclusion I have - you know the value of tax-free money and you will want to load up on it. Let's face it - tax-free puts us 20-40% ahead of the crowd before we've even gotten started. So where can wage earners find the money to stuff into their tax-free equity-indexed life insurance policy?

Here are 7 funding thoughts to get you started:

1.	Company-Sponsored tax-qualified plan contributions that exceed the employer's match as we've just discussed
2.	Your annual tax-refund. Rather than making an interest-free loan to Uncle Sam, change your withholdings, and re-allocate what would otherwise be a year-end tax refund, into monthly contributions to your tax-free wealth account.
3.	Old life insurance policy cash value. It can be rolled into a new policy tax-free, and become a source of starting a true wealth-building juggernaut.
4.	Mortgage Pre-Payment money. If you like to make extra principal payments on your mortgage, consider re-directing those dollars to your tax-free wealth account instead. Growing the same amount - tax-free, is likely to result in a greater accumulation of wealth than

	the cost of the tax-deductible mortgage interest you will continue to pay.
5.	Post-Penalty Strategic Rollout. Some people are so concerned about future taxation, it may make sense to take money out of their IRA over a few years, pay the taxes, and re-deploy the remainder into a tax-free wealth account. Qualified money that is re-deployed into an Indexed Universal Life policy creates access to insurance advances that can be used to pay the tax and/or penalty.
6.	IRS Rule 72t Rollout - this provision of the tax code allows you to take money out of an IRA penalty free (not tax-free) under certain conditions. Rolling it into a tax-free account makes a lot of sense in many cases.
7.	Emergency Fund - emergency funds recognize the need for instant liquidity. Using cash value life insurance as an emergency fund repository since it remains liquid (accessible), risk-free, and tax-free to boot.

Chapter 26

Plan "A" for the Qualified Plan Owner

Millions of people have accumulated wealth inside an IRA, 401(k), or other tax-qualified plan. And many of those who are in - or are approaching retirement, are starting to wonder - with good reason - whether the partnership they forged with Uncle Sam all those years ago was such a good idea after all.

In our Jack and Jill story a couple of chapters back, we saw an example of one saver who ignored conventional wisdom and paid taxes on the money she socked away. Over her investing lifetime, her "pay-as-you-go" tax bill was $40,000. Jack on the other hand, drank the qualified plan Kool-Aid, saved and invested the $40,000 rather than paying it to Uncle Sam, and at retirement, was staring into the face of a tax bill that he had successfully grown to $338,034. That's right, for the option to defer taxes of $40,000; he turned the eventual bill into more than 1/3 of a million dollars.

Jill paid her tax on the seed - Jack paid his on the harvest. And you don't have to be a farmer to understand which is the better deal.

Surely there's an option - a way out?

Unfortunately, there is not. A deal is a deal, and Uncle Sam is not the kind of partner who will re-negotiate. That leaves millions of Americans with their money trapped inside tax-qualified plans, and the regrets only become more gut-wrenching as one-by-one - they contemplate the consequences of their decision to make that deal in the first place.

Oh - it sounded good at the time. Why save less by paying taxes on your money first - when you can defer them and pay taxes way down the road? Besides, they said, you're likely to be in a much lower tax bracket in your lower earning retirement years.

Here is reality.

Fact: It is highly unlikely that your **tax bracket** will be lower in retirement. The theory was that the primary driver of tax rates - was income. Lower income in retirement would mean a lower tax rate, and therefore lower taxes. That theory ignores two very important considerations. First, tax rates are in perpetual motion. Every few years, a president - or congress, decides that tweaking the tax rates will be just what the country needs in order to remedy some problem-du-jour. Most times, those "adjustments" go in one direction - UP!

Even if they haven't gone up significantly yet - they're going to. It is an undeniable fact that future tax rates will be higher than they are today.

Fact 2: It is highly unlikely that your **taxes** will be lower in retirement. Not only will we be impacted by the tax rates - we'll be further impacted by the taxes themselves. The difference is the illusion of marginal versus effective tax rates (great - just what you wanted to know more about, right?). Let me make this as painless as possible, by using an example.

	Joe and Jane Worker	Joe and Jane Retiree
Annual Income	$100,000	$45,000
Deduction for Kids	$9,000	$0
Deduction for Home Mortgage	$15,000	$0
Other Deductions	$6,000	$1,000
Net Taxable Income	$70,000	$44,000
Tax	$9,750	$5,750
Effective Tax Rate (tax/income)	13.9%	13.1%
Marginal Tax Rate (tax on next $ of Income)	25%	15%

When the tax-qualified plan promoters make their case, they focus on the *marginal tax rate* - the rate at which the next dollar of income would be taxed. They'll tell Joe and Jane to put their money in a qualified plan because they'll defer taxes at a rate of 25%, and pay them at a rate of 15%.

That may turn out to be true. But for Joe and Jane in retirement, the kids are grown and can no longer be deducted, and the house is paid for so there is no more mortgage interest to deduct. That means their *effective* tax rate is almost identical in retirement - to what it was during their working years (13.9% while working, 13.1% when retired). They were led by the experts to focus on marginal rates rather than effective rates.

Fact 3: You can't defer taxes forever. While the idea may have been to start drawing an income from our qualified plan in retirement, many people find that they don't need that money. They've done well enough with other investments, perhaps have a pension, and find that, when combined with social security, their income is adequate to support their lifestyle without tapping the old qualified plan. They'd prefer to leave their qualified plan money alone. Let it keep growing - keep deferring the taxes - and maybe pass it on someday.

Sorry - Uncle Sam has decided that by the time we're 70-1/2 years old - he's waited long enough - and wants to start collecting his share. So he forces what are known as Required Minimum Distributions (RMD's). By forcing us to take at least some of our money out, it gets added to our tax return as income, and fully taxed. This can be particularly aggravating for those who don't need the money for lifestyle. Paying taxes is painful enough - but paying taxes on money we don't even need is downright maddening. Yet - this is part of the rule set we signed on to. It may not have been talked about much way back then (for obvious reasons), but it can become one of the most annoying realities many retirees face.

Fact 4: Qualified Plan Distributions Can/Will Trigger Taxes on Social Security Benefits. Most people believe social security benefits are not taxed. That's true - as long as you don't earn too much (according to the government) in retirement. But earning too much isn't just a function of whether we have a job in retirement; income taxes apply to income from "all sources," and that includes the money we take out of our qualified plan.

Let's revisit Joe and Jane Retiree from the example above. Their total retirement income was $45,000. Let's assume social security benefits made up $20,000 of that total and the remaining $25,000 came from money they drew from their IRA (which was converted from a former 401(k)). According to IRS rule, up to 50% of Joe and Jane's social security benefit is now taxable. Fifty percent of $20,000 is $10,000 X 15% (their marginal rate) = $1,500 in taxes on their social security income - *caused by their Required Minimum Distribution*!

Since Joe and Jane were well past 59-1/2 - they thought they escaped the 10% penalty for early withdrawal of qualified funds. They may have, but the tax they paid on their social security benefits - triggered because of those forced RMD's - made it seem as if the "penalty" would haunt them for the rest of their lives. Unfortunately, they're right. Seems like the government has "got-em" either way.

Want more bad news? If - one year, Joe needed a hip replacement, and the couple had to dip into the IRA for an extra $10,000 to pay the bill, up to 80% of Joe and Jane's social security benefit would be taxable - not the 50% that had been. They would have crossed another government-defined "affluence" tax threshold and the Social Security tax penalty would be even worse.

Fact 5: Two sure things in life are Death and Taxes. Except in this case - they go together. Some qualified plan owners think the way to beat the tax man at his own game is to die with a big whoppin' balance in the IRA. They reason that because there is an estate tax exemption, their IRA balance will pass tax-free, and they will have put one over on Unc.

No such luck. We get one "free pass" so long as it's to a spouse. If Joe dies before Jane, she will get the keys to Joe's IRA without a tax consequence. The problem is that when Jane passes away - the whole enchilada is taxable - in the year of her death.

How so? Even if it escapes the estate tax (which is far from a sure bet), we have to remember that the money in the IRA has never been income-taxed - not a single penny of it. So here's how it works.

Let's assume Joe and Jane made June and John - their two adult children - 50% beneficiaries of their estate, including $200,000 that remained in Joe and Jane's IRA. So June and John each inherit $100,000 (in addition to whatever other assets may have been passed on). That $100,000 is *added* to their regular earned income that year, and they are taxed on the total. So if John made $40,000 that year, he would be taxed as if he had made $140,000 the year of his inheritance. If Jane made $95,000 that year - she would be taxed on $195,000 of total income.

Before the inheritance, June's income put her in the 25% marginal tax bracket, and John was in the 15% bracket. But now, June is thrust into the 33% bracket, and John to the 28% bracket. That means June will pay an additional $7,600 on her regular income - and John will pay an extra $5,200 on his. And that's in addition to the 33% and 25% respectively they'll pay on their $100,000 inheritance.

Okay - so maybe it's hard to feel too sorry for June and John. After all - they did just inherit a bunch of money even if it is taxed. But what about Joe and Jane? They may be singing with the angels now, but do you think they intended or anticipated that $78,300 - nearly 40% of the value of their remaining life's financial legacy - would go to Uncle Sam - with just the after-tax balance going to their children and grandchildren?

Most families never learn this lesson until it is forced upon them when it's too late and there is no retreat - no option to even minimize the damage. They're locked into a fate that was pre-determined - even if unconsciously and innocently.

There is one other tax consideration we have to acknowledge. Estate and inheritance taxes could make the outcome even worse. The Federal Government assesses Estate taxes, but "inheritance taxes" are their equivalent levied by the state. Many states don't have an inheritance tax - but many others do.

At least at the federal level, there is an estate tax exemption - a threshold under which the estate tax is waived. Many state inheritance taxes are tied to the federal estate tax, meaning that exemption threshold applies at the state level, too. However some states either have no exemption, or their exemption is different than the federal exemption.

Without getting into the nuances of estate and inheritance taxes, know this: the combination of income, estate, and inheritance taxes can consume up to 80% of any qualified plan money that is passed on if no planning is put in place while the estate owner(s) are living. That's the highest rate of taxation in the entire tax code - and for a reason - the dead can no longer object.

Please, please, please - get with an estate-planning attorney while you can. See what the implications are for you, and take appropriate measures. The good news is that there are planning strategies that can eliminate most - even all of the potential pitfalls of estate and inheritance taxes - and the few dollars you may spend in legal fees, will have the greatest return on investment of anything you can do.

Rescue Your Retirement from the Ravages of All Taxation. I want to lay out a plan for you that will cost you nothing other than the price of this book. The good news is that what we're about to explore will save you tens - even hundreds of thousands in taxes should you choose to heed the advice.

Let's look at the pre-retiree first. Perhaps you're in your 40's or 50's, and the underbelly realities of your qualified plan have suddenly been put into words. You want a way out - a way off the merry-go-round of the tax time bomb you've been building. You want out of that qualified plan. You want a do-over.

You have 15-20 years until retirement. You've accumulated $500,000 in a company 401(k) - which - at retirement, will be rolled over into an IRA. Step one is to STOP THE INSANITY. Stop contributing money to the tax-deferred plan. Start putting the same money into a tax-free plan - I've been telling you about one in the last several chapters. If you're getting a big employer match, I'll make an exception - but don't put a penny into the plan more than is necessary to get the maximum amount of free money (matching contributions) from your employer. If you're saving at a higher rate than that - which I hope you are - get the next dollar and all the dollars that follow - into a tax-free plan.

Now all we have to deal with is the money you've already accumulated in the 401(k) plan. First, realize that the tax that's due on that $500,000 is inescapable. What we need to do is figure a way to deal with it in the most efficient manner possible - and that doesn't mean taking it all out at once. An underutilized section of the IRS code known as a 72t rollout can be used to extract yourself from the qualified plan. This rule let's you take a series of distributions over your "life expectancy" without incurring the 10% early withdrawal penalty. There are a number of simple calculators available on the web to determine how much can be taken in 72t distributions, one of which is: http://www.bankrate.com/calculators/retirement/72-t-distribution-calculator.aspx. You may not have a 72t rollout option while you're still employed by the sponsoring employer, but you will if you change jobs; and more employers (in order to escape the legal liability their plans are imposing on them) will allow an "in-service" rollover option.

In round numbers, a 50 year-old 401(k) owner with $500,000 in a tax-deferred plan can take about $25,000 per year out in 72t, penalty-free distributions. That $25,000 is added to his other income, and if he's in the 28% marginal tax bracket, he'll have an additional tax bill of $7,000 each year. Remember, that tax liability has always been there - it's just been sleeping inside the 401(k) plan - so this is not a new tax, just one we've decided to extinguish now rather than later (at a potentially higher rate).

Now let's make some magic happen. If we put that $25,000 a year 72t rollout into a cash value life insurance policy, we can take advances against the death benefit any time we want with a simple phone call. That money comes out of the death benefit, while the $25,000 premium deposit (less the cost of insurance) continues to grow at the index rate with no risk.

So on April 1 - two weeks before taxes are due - call the insurance company and ask for a $7,000 advance. *In other words, let's pay the tax because we have to - but let's do it with the insurance company's money - not our own.*

Next year - and the year after - and the year after that - we do the exact same thing. Paying taxes is no fun - but paying them with OPM (other people's money) may actually border on fun!

But what if you're already retired - what options do you have? The same basic strategy can work even better if you're already retired - even if you're over 70-1/2 and are being forced to pay taxes on RMD's you don't need to support your lifestyle. The added benefit you have is that you no longer need to use the 72t method of taking distributions since you're out of the penalty phase (i.e. older than 59-1/2).

We can either move the money into the cash-value life insurance policy in one lump sum, or we can move it over the course of 5 years or more. However we move it out - taxes will be due on the amount taken out, so I typically recommend doing so over at least 5 years.

So the first year, we take out $110,000, leaving $390,000 in the qualified plan. Why $110,000? Because the $390,00 will continue to grow, and we should be able to safely anticipate a total of $50,000 of growth over the time we're moving it into the life insurance platform - for a total of $550,000 going into the Insurance plan over 5 years.

Taxes on the $110,000 could be as much as $30,000. So we go to the insurance company to get a $30,000 advance against the life insurance benefit, and pay Uncle Sam with the insurance company's money. If we ever need to take more to supplement our lifestyle needs, we can - tax-free - and if we don't - we'll pass on a tax-free death benefit that could top $1,000,000 - or more.

While it's true that a $500,000 IRA balance could grow to $1,000,000 over the same time, the heirs could be left with $700,000 on the high side - or as little as $200,000 on the low end, because of federal and state income taxes, estate taxes, and inheritance taxes. Wouldn't $1,000,000 tax-free be better than $700,000 - and a whole lot better than $200,000?

Finally, take comfort in this. In our previous conversation about the merits of cash value life insurance, we characterized an insurance policy as a contract rather than an investment. We talked about the value of a contract being a defined outcome for our money rather than an at-risk outcome. But additionally, contracts are not subject to probate. A judge cannot decide where the contract value goes - the terms of the contract prevail - and those terms include your designation of a beneficiary(ies) that only you can change. So long-lost, but crazy cousin Seymour - who goes to the judge and tries to convince him that you had always intended to leave 50% of your estate to him - gets shut down when it comes to life insurance proceeds.

As a contract, its value may not be included for purposes of Medicaid qualification. A contract isn't included as an asset when determining qualifications for student aid and government-backed student loans. And there are other features that make life insurance an excellent vehicle for asset-protection purposes.

One word of caution - an insurance contract stops being a contract and turns into an asset at the death of the insured. So often times, life insurance is held in an ILIT - Irrevocable Life Insurance Trust. That way, when the contract converts into cash (at the death of the insured), it too is excluded from the estate - and therefore can also escape estate - and inheritance taxes. This is a very important consideration for those with large estates.

ILITs are easy to set up, easy to administer, and inexpensive compared to the estate tax implications that could otherwise eat up a portion of the death benefit.

Chapter 27

The Five Money Needs - Revisited

Earlier in this book I introduced the concept of the Five Money Needs. Before that, we learned what we didn't want - market risk, taxes, and fees and commissions. The Five Money Needs gave us a framework for what we do want: Safety, Growth, Income, Liquidity, and Tax-Efficiency. We then laid out a wealth-building plan that combined the guarantee of an equity-indexed money contract with a life insurance policy - both of which are available in the same product - equity-indexed universal life insurance.

Now that we've seen and studied the mechanics of how each of the components work, both individually and in concert with one another, let's take a look at how they stack up against what we said we wanted, needed, and what we agreed would almost guarantee a successful outcome - the Five Money Needs.

Safety

Is an equity-indexed life insurance policy safe? We have to look at safety in three different ways. First, let's consider the life insurance industry itself. How safe is it as a whole? Following is a very good article on the subject.

How Safe is a Life Insurance/Annuity Company?

Through devastating world wars, financial recessions and depressions, sweeping epidemics, earthquakes and fires, inflation and deflation, the life insurance industry has protected people to a degree unmatched by any type of financial institution in the history of the world.

Today the life insurance industry provides more than a trillion dollars of death protection to American consumers.

The financial reliability of the life insurance industry, even in times of financial panic, was demonstrated convincingly during the Great Depression of 1929-38 when some 9,000 banks suspended operations while 99% of all life insurance in force continued unaffected. Reinsurance, acquisitions, and mergers protected virtually all policy owners in the affected companies against personal loss.

The State Insurance Department

The State Insurance Department is a most vital department in each of our fifty states. Acting on its own state's insurance laws and regulations, it supervises all aspects of an insurance company's operation within that state. In addition, the State Insurance Department licenses all companies and agents to sell insurance within its boundaries. It must also approve all policy forms and in some cases, sales materials before they can be offered to the public. The Departments review complaints from consumers and mergers of companies that do business within its boundaries.

Required Reserves Ensure Payment of Policyholder Benefits

A large percentage of each premium dollar calculated by actuaries for each company goes into the policy owner's reserve fund. This policy reserve (Legal Reserve) fund is a liability to the life insurance company. The fund is established as a way of determining or measuring the assets the company must maintain in order to be able to meet its future commitments under the policies it has issued.

The reserve liabilities are established as financial safeguards to ensure the company will have sufficient assets to pay its claims and other commitments when they fall due. These assets are kept intact for payment of living and death benefits to the insured. Life companies that comply with the legal reserve requirements established by the state insurance laws are known as legal reserve life insurance companies.

Periodic Company Examinations

Every year all legal reserve life insurance companies submit annual statements to the insurance departments of each state in which they are licensed to do business. The format and contents of the forms used are prescribed by the State Insurance Commissioners and they are a detailed report of an insurance company's financial status that is important in evaluating the company's solvency and compliance with the insurance laws.

Every few years, depending on a company's home state law, all companies operating in more than one state undergo a detailed home office zone examination of its financial position. This audit is conducted by a team of State Insurance Department Examiners representing the various zones in which the company is licensed to do business. Companies licensed in only one state are subject only to an annual home office examination by their State Insurance Department.

Additional Security Safeguards

1. Reinsurance: Nearly every legal reserve life insurance company further protects its policyholders by reinsuring part of the coverage with a life reinsurance company. This is done when the company will not or cannot undertake a risk alone. Reinsurance prevents relatively sizeable claims from depleting a company's policyholder reserves. The amount reinsured depends on many factors such as the size of the individual claim and the number of claims a company can expect.

2. Surplus: The surplus is the amount by which a company's assets exceed its liabilities. The surplus protects the policyholders and third parties against any deficiency in the insurer's provisions for meeting its obligations. The determination of the optimum amount of surplus that a company will retain must be based on experience, current conditions, and an

awareness of the primary goal of maintaining a strong company that is always able to pay claims as they arise.

Mergers

In the unlikely event that a company's annual statement or its own examination reveals possible financial weakness, one of several avenues is open to the company: (1) Produce additional operating capital; (2) Sell its business to another life company; (3) Merge into another financially stable life company. A legal reserve life insurance company simply does not close its doors and go out of business declaring that all policies are null and void. Legal reserve life policyholders enjoy personal security safeguards unknown by other types of business.

Yours for Life

Another unique advantage of legal reserve life insurance is that if one company is purchased or merged into another, there is no change whatsoever in the policy benefits or premiums. Legal reserve life insurance companies have established a public responsibility to respect both the letter and the spirit of laws and regulations so the interests of their policyholders are always protected.

Policyholders Protection Comes First

Today, as has been the case for many years, it is unlikely for the policy owner of legal reserve life insurance companies to lose their policy benefits. Through strict state insurance department regulations, the establishment of many state insurance guaranty associations and because of the insurance industry's history of financial stability and public responsibility to operate in a manner not detrimental to the welfare of the community, your policy is secured by industry safeguards.

As for individual life insurance companies, there are several credit agencies that report on the financial soundness of insurance companies, including Moody's, A.M. Best, Fitch, Standard & Poors, and others. These companies give report card-like grades from A+ - down. My personal recommendation is to avoid companies with a rating lower than A.

Finally, there is one other internal "risk" in an insurance policy, and that's the cost of the pure life insurance. Buried in the fine print of the policy is the insurance company's option to set - and potentially increase the cost of insurance. An increase in the cost of insurance would suppress policy earnings and over time, compromise its ability to build wealth.

This option is there to protect the insurance company in the event of a human catastrophe like a medical epidemic or widespread disaster of some kind. However, we should note that most insurance companies have never increased their cost of insurance. The simple reason is that life expectancies continue to expand, not contract. Even in the remote event of an increase in mortality charges, the policy still allows options, like reducing the amount of pure insurance (death benefit) so that the proportion of premium dollars going into the money contract account versus the insurance account, remains the same as before the cost of insurance increased.

I'm often asked about AIG - the mega-insurance company that was the subject of the early 2009 $780 billion government bailout (that also included GM, Chrysler, and many of the large investment banks). Isn't that an example of an insurance company essentially failing? My first response is to point out that AIG is a conglomeration of several different kinds of companies, including insurance entities that have nothing to do with Life Insurance. In fact, American General Insurance - AIG's life insurance arm, was, and continues to be the crown jewel of the AIG empire from a fiscal performance point of view. What got AIG in trouble was insuring many of the mortgage defaults that happened after the government-contrived housing bubble burst. It had nothing to do with their life insurance operation; and in fact had AIG been allowed to fail, the life insurance arm would have emerged unscathed *because* it is regulated by the insurance commissioners of each state - and it is likely that AIG policy owners would have suffered no losses. Two other quick points. AIG has since repaid the taxpayer every nickel that was lent to it during the bailout; and I'm not sure it's a bad thing to have a business that holds my money declared "too big to fail." Isn't that like the federal government giving a guarantee to a private company and its customers/policyholders?

I remain comfortable to this day with anybody who owns an American General Life policy or annuity.

Conclusion: on the safety front, there is not much out there that could top an insurance company on the safety scale. I've argued with banker friends in the past that insurance companies are safer than banks. From a pure balance sheet point of view, I win hands down. The trump card they always play is their FDIC insurance. When I point out that the state guaranty funds (see article above) are the insurance industry's equivalent of FDIC insurance - and that the state guaranty funds are funded with real money - not digital entries in a government ledger somewhere - I can usually close the case.

Growth
It should be clear by now that the growth feature of equity-indexed life insurance is one of its most exciting features.

- Every policy offers a fixed rate option that is usually about a 4-5X multiple of what is available from bank CDs.

- The equity-indexed option creates the opportunity for earnings that are more in line with stock market performance.

- A wide variety of crediting options (floor and cap, spread, participation rate) coupled with a wide variety of indices (S&P 500, Dow, EuroStoxx, Heng Seng, etc.) provide excellent investment strategy options for policy owners.

- And the ability to mix and match crediting methods (part in the fixed account, part in the equity-indexed account) makes them ultimately flexible for even the most sophisticated investor.

So how does equity-indexed life insurance stack up on the growth-scale? Outstanding.

Income

Quite simply, there is nothing that will produce as much income per dollar of account value as a cash value life insurance policy. That's because as we begin to draw income out of our policy, we do so through the policy loan feature which does not deplete our money contract account. On the contrary - since the money we're using for income is coming from the insurance company's account, our money contract continues to benefit from the same growth in our retirement years, that it did during our accumulation years.

There is no other account, investment, or financial institution that will make that deal with us - and the sole reason an insurance company can is because the insurance benefit is there to extinguish all the borrowed money, plus interest - guaranteed, without recourse.

In terms of the inexhaustibility of income, an annuity is the only instrument that can outperform a life insurance policy because the insurance company is taking on the longevity risk by guaranteeing income continuation even if the annuity account is depleted. An annuity won't produce as much income for the same reason, but the income guarantee may be the more important feature for some.

In constructing an income payout from a life insurance policy, a prudent insurance professional will ask the insurance company software to calculate your income payment as if it had to last to at least age 100. Some will even request income to age 121. In doing so - even though those income payments rely on continuing policy performance (growth inside the policy), income is as close to guaranteed as it can be - short of an outright guarantee.

Because the income feature is so close to guaranteed, and because it will produce more income than any other instrument out there - the income feature of a properly structured equity-indexed life insurance policy is unbeatable.

Liquidity

When we talk about liquidity, we talk about how quickly we can convert an asset into cash, and how much it costs us to do so. By that pure definition, an insurance policy can be converted into cash as quickly as just about any other investment (stock, bond, mutual fund, CD).

One measure of liquidity that the mainstreamers often use to attack insurance products (life insurance and annuities) is what is known as Surrender Charge.

These are the insurance company's version of the "loads" and investing fees we've talked about in the mainstream world. An insurance company is entitled to recover their cost of sales somehow - just as are the mainstreamers. The insurance industry does it with surrender charges - and I believe this is the best way to recover those sales charges. It is also what is in your best interest as a consumer.

Let me make the case this way. In the mainstream world, sales commissions/loads and management fees (from fee-based planners) are either deducted from the principal we put in up front, or they're charged on the exit value when we sell a position - sometimes both.

When they're assessed up front, they have the effect of requiring that the investment grow just to get us back to break even. When they're charged on the back end, they can grow unchecked. Neither is ideal.

In contrast, the insurance company calculates and locks in the sales cost on the beginning balance (there are some nominal costs on subsequent premium contributions), then recovers the cost of sales a little bit at a time - rather than all up front - or all on the back end. This leaves more of the dollars we put into the policy, working for us, growing and compounding in our money contract account.

Because sales costs are recovered over time, insurance companies impose a "surrender" charge on the policy - which *only applies* if the policy is terminated before the insurance company has fully recovered those costs.

If not fully recovered by the time a policy is cancelled, the surrender charge reduces the amount refunded to the policy-owner by the unrecovered portion of the sales costs. If the policy remains in force, the surrender fades away each year until the insurer's sales costs are fully recovered, at which point the surrender charge disappears altogether.

Consider this:

- $10,000 going into a mutual fund with a front-end load of 5% means that our account value is only $9,500 on day one.

- $10,000 going into an investment that assesses a 5% back-end fee means the sales charge has no limit. If our account value doubles to $20,000 - and we sell - the 5% back-end fee costs $1,000 - twice what it would have cost if it were front-loaded.

- An insurance charge of 5% ($500) might be recovered at a rate of 1/2% per year over 10 years (to keep the comparison apples-to-apples). That means $9,950 would be working (more than with the front-end load); and with no back-end fee, the charge is limited and defined up front. If we surrendered the policy after one year, the insurance company would reduce our money contract account balance by the $450 sales cost they had not yet recovered. But even if we absorbed a surrender charge at any point during those first 10 years and took our balance - we would have more money with a surrender charge than without one - and we'd be better off in the long run because of the benefit of more money working and compounding in all of those early years.

The truth is that a life insurance policy is liquid at all times. The amount that it can be liquidated for might be less in the early years; and taking the full amount out might trigger a tax, but the same would apply to any other investment or investment account; so the liquidity features of a cash value life insurance policy are excellent - and very competitive.

Tax-Efficiency
This one is short and sweet. There is simply no vehicle on the planet that provides more tax-efficiency than a cash value life insurance policy - period. That's because you simply can't do better than tax-free.

We put after-tax deposits into the policy. They grow (technically) tax-deferred. If we take money out in the form of policy loans, we're taking it out tax-free. And when we pass on what's left in the policy via the death benefit - it too passes income tax-free. And when the policy is held in an ILIT, it can also pass estate and inheritance tax-free.

One question that comes up from time to time is: How long does the insurance industry think it can hold on to its tax-free advantage? Could it change? That's a very insightful question, and deserves a good answer - which I'll break into two parts.

First, it has changed - three times in history. Each of those acts of congress we mentioned earlier, DEFRA, TEFRA, and TAMRA, addressed the tax-free question, but they did so in an interesting way. Rather than attacking the tax-free nature of life insurance, they instead raised the ratio of pure life insurance a policy owner must have in relationship to the proportion of premium dollars going into the money contract side of the ledger.

Before those regulations, the rich and famous would purchase as little pure life insurance as possible - and jam as much cash into the money contract account as possible. These policies were extremely efficient because with little pure insurance, they were very inexpensive. Congress thought - and rightfully so - that the ratio of insurance to cash was so out of balance that insurance contracts were looking a lot more like disguised investment accounts than life insurance policies; so the three acts of congress raised the bar in terms of the ratio of life insurance to cash.

That should tell us a couple of things. First - it could happen again. If history prevails however, all policies that preceded the new regulations were grandfathered in, and were unaffected by the new regulations. So just like paying taxes at today's known rates is safer than deferring them and gambling on tomorrow's rates - my suggestion is to lock in a policy TODAY, rather than risking another government-imposed increase in the insurance requirement somewhere down the line.

More importantly, these government-imposed minimums tell us how powerful and valuable these policies are. Anything that congress wants to limit our access to means it is good for us - and not so good for them. So load up!

The other point to remember is that it is not some regulation or law that is exclusive to the life insurance industry that makes our withdrawals tax-free. Rather, it is that we are not taking our own money out of our policy - we're borrowing from the insurance company and the insurance company's account.

For congress to eliminate that benefit, they'd have to tax all borrowed money - meaning when we secure a mortgage - there would be a tax; when we finance a car - there would be a tax; when we charge something to our credit card - there would be a tax. Now I wouldn't put anything past our government when it comes to taxation - but that one is so unlikely as to be considered absurd.

Summary

Cash value life insurance - and equity-indexed universal life insurance in particular, meets all Five Money Needs - it meets them all at the same time - and it delivers a quantity of each that should be compelling to even the most skeptical investor.

In my 30 plus years in the money world, I have yet to find anyone that can show me something that better meets the Five Money Needs. If we agree that we want these five things - we want them all - we want them at the same time; and that by having them, our chances of succeeding at the wealth building game are almost certain, we should demand them. And now we know we can have them - uniquely - with life insurance.

My challenge to you is that even if you're skeptical of what I've laid out here - get your 401(k) statement, your IRA statement, or your brokerage statement out. Look at each of the investments you hold and make your own assessment of how well - or not so well - they stack up against the Five Money Needs.

After you've done that - schedule a meeting with your advisor. Tell them how you've assessed your portfolio against the Five Money Needs and ask two questions.

1. How would their assessment compare to yours?
2. What investments can they put into your account that meet all Five Money Needs - at the same time?

I'm pretty sure I know what you'll discover - a blank stare.

Rigged

Chapter 28

Give ... til it Doesn't Hurt

It's Christmas morning. You've had your coffee, chatted a bit, passed on the fruitcake, and now it's time for the fun part - it's time to get down to the business of opening presents. Suddenly, there's that awkward, "who goes first" moment.

Let me ask you a question. Would you rather open a present with your name on it - or watch someone else open a present that's from you?

I ask that question to people all the time because I think it reveals the nature of man. If you're over age 10, nearly 100% of you would choose to be the *giver* over the *recipient*. How can that make sense? Opening a present always results in a personal gain. Giving a present to another always results in a personal loss. Why would we choose the loss - over the gain?

Because life is about much more than gaining and winning. Life is about giving to others. Life is about being a blessing to the world. Happiness is measured by how much we give - not how much we gain. And where does that come from? How is it that we can spend so much acquiring and building wealth, yet we get our greatest warm and fuzzies when we give it away?

I believe giving is in our DNA. I believe we are givers by nature - because we're made in the image of the greatest giver of all - God. Whether you're a believer or not, it's hard to escape the reality that giving provides us with meaning and purpose. The more we give, the more meaning and purpose we have in our lives.

If you feel the same way - I have some really good news. We can take what we've learned in these pages, and do more of what our souls crave - and that's to give to others.

When we look at giving purely as a financial transaction, there is one winner, and one loser. If we give, we lose financially, and the recipient wins - financially. If we withhold (don't give), we win financially, and the cause that asked us to give - loses - financially. But as we just said, giving is much more than a cold, emotionless financial transaction - so thankfully, giving takes place in our world. In fact, it takes place in our country in greater proportion than in any other country in the world. When we look at giving as an emotional transaction, it suddenly becomes a win-win, and that's why giving happens. The emotional win-win trumps the financial win-lose.

But what if we could make the financial side of a giving transaction a win-win too? What if we could eliminate the tug-o-war between the emotional win-win, and the financial win-lose? Could we change the world?

Absolutely. And here's how.

Remember that in our discussion of cash value life insurance, when we set up the life insurance account, we're able to begin drawing advances against it and use the money for whatever purpose we choose. When we do so, we are not drawing from or otherwise disturbing our money contract account. We talked about some examples of how we could use that money. We talked about using these advances as a tax-free, lifetime income stream. We also talked about using them to pay the tax bill when converting a qualified plan into a tax-free plan.

So why not use advances on the life insurance account as a source of money we give to charity? That's right - we can protect, grow, and compound the money in our money contract account - _and_ give insurance company money to charities by taking advances on the life insurance account. We can do it monthly - all at one-time - or we can even designate that a portion of the life insurance account go to charity(ies) at our death. Now that's a financial win-win. And our gift is still tax-deductible under current tax law.

Life insurance has long been used as a planned gift - a gift after death. With equity-indexed life insurance, we can do both - we can give during our lifetime, and we can give after we're gone.

For me personally, this is one of the most important points of this entire book, because I believe we can change the world by applying the very lessons that can lead to personal financial success - to do the same thing for those causes that touch us and that meet human needs.

Appendix 1

Show Me The Money

Background

This is Jack's story. Jack knew that as an investor, he had to make well thought-out, wise investing decisions, aided by the help of a professional advisor - in order to build wealth over time. It was just common sense. But instinctively he also knew that the job was even more critical because his account would have to grow fast enough to overcome three factors that were working against him - three factors that would get paid long before he ever would.

- **Market-Risk** would steal from him from time to time in the form of losses on individual investments as well as overall market gyrations.

- **Fees and commissions** charged by his advisor, his advisor's firm, the mutual funds, account managers, custodians, and others in the wealth building "food chain" - most of whom would be paid whether Jack's account grew or not.

- **Taxes** would take their share. As they say - "the two sure things in life are death and taxes."

While everything he read, listened to, and gathered from others he trusted had convinced him that these were just part of the game - "the price of poker" - as one friend put it - he knew in his gut they were huge obstacles his account had to crest before he would ever benefit from a dime's worth of his efforts.

So he set out to analyze just how much of a drain on the growth of his account these three might take. He wanted to know the real cost - not just shrug it off to "part of the game." He wanted a constant reminder of just how critical his decisions were - and how much he needed to attend to his own affairs - even with professional help. At the end of the day, others might play a role that influenced his results; sometimes positive - sometimes not - but *he* was the one who would have to live with the outcome - whichever way it fell.

Jack's First Decision

Many of Jack's colleagues used tax-qualified plans like IRAs, 401(k)s, SEPs, and others - to build their wealth. The argument was that there would be more dollars growing if those dollars weren't taxed in the first place. If Jack earned a buck and wanted to save and invest it - he could put the whole dollar into a qualified account - but if it was in a taxable account, he might be left with only - $.80 or so after taxes.

Of course tax qualified plans don't eliminate the taxes - they only defer them into the future. And Jack knows that as his account grows - so will his tax liability. And unlike a taxable account - where investments that are held more than a year qualify for the lower capital gains tax rate - there's no such deal with tax qualified plans. Every penny will be taxed as ordinary income as withdrawn - the highest rate in the tax code.

He also knows that qualified plans will be taxed at future tax rates - not today's rates. That would be a good deal if future taxes rates were predicted to be lower than current ones - but Jack can't construct a single argument to convince himself that future taxes will be anything but higher - perhaps much higher.

Finally, he knows there are as many mainstream arguments in favor of tax-qualified plans as there are against them. And if there are arguments on both sides - it must mean that there is no clear-cut winner when it comes to the after-tax outcome. So he decides to conduct his analysis both ways.

The Impact of Losses

The first thing Jack wants to understand is the impact the risk of losses might have on his wealth plan. He knows the "rule of 72" which explains the power of compound interest. It says that by dividing an interest rate into 72, we can know how long it will take to double our money. So at a 7.2% rate of growth, money will double in 10 years (72 ÷ 7.2 = 10 years).

To prove the point - the first column in the table below shows a $1,000 deposit building to $2,000 over the course of 10 years, when grown at 7.2% per annum.

It's the second column however, that gets Jack's attention. He wants to know what the impact of a small setback would be. In other words -

what would happen if his string of 7.2% earning years was interrupted with a - 5% loss in - say - year three (highlighted). Losses certainly happen - and probably many times over an investing lifetime. They happen with individual investments - and they happen to entire accounts when markets move in a negative direction.

Year	7.2%	7.2%
0	$1,000	$1,000
1	$1,072	$1,072
2	$1,149	$1,149
3	$1,232	$1,092
4	$1,321	$1,120
5	$1,416	$1,255
6	$1,518	$1,345
7	$1,627	$1,442
8	$1,744	$1,546
9	$1,870	$1,657
10	$2,000	$1,776
		-224

The dollar difference at the end of 10 years is $224 - not terribly dramatic. But less obvious is the difference in percentage terms. It's 12.6% less money. In other words, that one small, 5% loss creates an outcome difference of 12.6% less money in the end.

What's even more revealing, is the **permanence** of that loss. When Jack takes both 10-year ending balances, and doubles each over succeeding 10-year periods well into the future - stunningly - the 12.6% loss proves permanent.

Year	10% Compound	10% Compound	Difference
10	$2,000	$1,776	-12.6%
20	$4,000	$3,552	-12.6%
30	$8,000	$7,104	-12.6%
40	$16,000	$14,208	-12.6%
50	$32,000	$28,416	-12.6%

No one had ever shown Jack the math of losses this way before. And it meant two things. First, that losses are far greater than he had believed. He thought a 5% loss was a 5% loss. Now he sees that a 5% loss really is a 12.6% loss. What's more, that can never be recovered. Once it's incurred, it's permanent.

He has always been taught to focus on the *dollar balance* in his account. Who could argue that turning $1,000 into $28,416 over 50 years was a bad thing? It's not - it's a great thing - *until we know, that had he avoided that loss in the first place - Jack would have had 12.6% more money in his account.*

He began to ask himself - what would 12.6% mean to his retirement lifestyle, how he would be able to support his charitable aspirations, and what he might pass on to the next generation. What if the difference wasn't $224, but $224,000? What's more, how many 5% losses had he already sustained in his brief "investing" lifetime - some of which were worse - far worse than a mere 5%?

Jack would never look at losing money the same way again. He was young. He would occasionally "swing for the fences" with his investments - thinking that was the way to get ahead. Besides - he had plenty of time to "make up for a few setbacks." Now he knew differently - he could *never* make up for *any* setback. He resolved then and there to take safety a whole lot more seriously and seek out advisors and investments that would minimize - even eliminate his exposure to irrecoverable losses - ever again.

First Pass
Things were really starting to get interesting for Jack. What else had he come to believe that perhaps had a different twist than what all his mainstream teaching and wisdom had convinced him was fact?

So he began to dive deeper. The next thing Jack wanted to do was to see what his outcome would be if he didn't have to absorb the negative earnings drain of losses, fees/commissions, and taxes.

What would happen if he invested $500/month - ($6,000 per year); grew his account by 10% compounded annually; and continued on that path for 35 years - from age 30, to age 65? The table below shows the results:

Year	Beginning Balance	New Savings	Ending Bal @10%
1	0	$6,000	$6,600
2	$6,600	$6,000	$13,860
3	$13,860	$6,000	$21,846
4	$21,846	$6,000	$30,631
5	$30,631	$6,000	$40,294
6	$40,294	$6,000	$50,923
7	$50,923	$6,000	$62,515
8	$62,515	$6,000	$75,477
9	$89,625	$6,000	$89,625
10	$105,187	$6,000	$105,187
11	$105,187	$6,000	$122,306
12	$122,306	$6,000	$141,136
13	$141,136	$6,000	$161,850
14	$161,850	$6,000	$184,635
15	$184,635	$6,000	$209,698
16	$209,698	$6,000	$237,698
17	$237,698	$6,000	$267,595
18	$267,595	$6,000	$300,955
19	$300,955	$6,000	$337,650
20	$337,650	$6,000	$378,015
21	$378,015	$6,000	$422,416
22	$422,416	$6,000	$471,258
23	$471,258	$6,000	$524,984
24	$524,984	$6,000	$584,082
25	$584,082	$6,000	$649,091
26	$649,091	$6,000	$720,600
27	$720,600	$6,000	$799,260

28	$799,260	$6,000	$885,786
29	$885,786	$6,000	$980,964
30	$980,964	$6,000	$1,085,661
31	$1,085,661	$6,000	$1,200,827
32	$1,200,827	$6,000	$1,327,509
33	$1,327,509	$6,000	$1,466,860
34	$1,466,860	$6,000	$1,620,146
35	$1,620,146	$6,000	**$1,788,761**

Jack was impressed - and encouraged. He could surely put away $500/month. It wouldn't be easy - but the idea of retiring with nearly $1.8 million was pretty attractive. He had visions of golf, travel, and the finer things of life for himself and his family.

But he wasn't getting too excited because he knew this number would shrink - perhaps significantly as he set out to determine what the impact of "the big three" as he was now calling them - really was. But now he had his baseline - so let the analysis begin!

The Impact of Losses - Part II

The next thing Jack wanted to do was to apply what he had just learned about the impact of losses - to his new 35-year spreadsheet. No question, he was resolved to becoming more diligent about avoiding losses - but he couldn't control the markets - and he knew there would be bumps in the road along the way. So he took three years and interrupted his 35-year string of 10% compound growth:

- In year 14, he changed his 10% growth - to flat - +/- zero
- In year 22, he replaced his 10% growth rate with a 5% loss
- In year 32, he changed his 10% growth - to flat - +/- zero - once again

Almost afraid to see the result - he was devastated to see his new bottom line shrivel to:

$1,328,926

That was **$450,000 less** than the $1.8 million he would have had without breaking his string of 10% earning years. Are you kidding? He checked his math - but the figures didn't change. Even more disconcerting was that his "interruptions" were pretty docile in comparison to history. In 2008 for example, the market tumbled 40% in one year. All he had accounted for was two flat years, and one year with a 5% loss. What would it look like if we had a 2008 again - or even more flat or down years?

He couldn't bring himself to even do the calculations. But if he was resolved to avoid losses after his simple analysis, he was even more resolute now.

The Impact of Fees and Commissions

Next, Jack set out to see what the impact of fees and commissions were. This was the one "wealth-eroder" he was the least afraid of. In the scheme of things, fees and commissions seemed pretty insignificant. But what was a reasonable figure for fees and commissions? He spent more time researching the subject than he anticipated - and the more he learned - the more confused he became.

- There were the $7.00/trade guys - but that was far from the whole story. There were account fees - custodial fees, and all sorts of other nickel-and-dime ways they chipped up their "take."

- There were "fee-only" advisors. The customary fee seemed to range from 1% on the low end (for a large account), and up to 2-3% for smaller accounts - like his. But even that wasn't the whole story. Mutual funds for example - even held in a fee-only account - have front-end loads, back-end "12-B-1" fees, expense ratios - all of which are like a double charge to his account.

- And when Jack looked at the fees associated with tax-qualified plans, the story really got murky. Turns out - those fees and commissions are almost impossible to know. He found a *60 Minutes* expose on YouTube that was positively terrifying. And when he went to the Department of Labor website to get their take, he found 22 different fees and commissions that could apply to qualified plans. Here's what else it said:

"Assume you are an employee with 35 years until retirement and a 401(k) account balance of $25,000. If returns on investments average 7 percent over the next 35 years; and fees

and expenses reduce your returns by 0.5 percent, your account will grow to $227,000. If fees and expenses are 1.5 percent however, your account balance will grow to only $163,000. The 1 percent difference in fees and expenses would reduce your account balance by 28%."

He also found that new legislation requires the full disclosure of fees - and the financial services industry is braced for impact. Furthermore, it seems the legal community smells blood in the water - and is beginning to sue large employers over the fees associated with their plans. Big names like Caterpillar, General Dynamics, Kraft Foods, even Wal-Mart have already settled class actions suits over fees and expenses.

Weighing all his evidence, Jack decided to conduct his analysis using a rate of 1.5% to represent all the various fees and commissions. Even though many fees were flat charges, 1.5% seemed reasonable. Some folks might do a bit better - some will pay 3% - even more. He wanted to use a justifiable number just to see what it revealed.

So he took his "untarnished" table - the one that had dangled the $1.8 million figure under his nose - and added a column to deduct fees and commissions at 1.5% of his annual account total each year.

Year	Beginning Balance	New Savings	1.5% Fees & Commissions	Ending Bal After Fees
1	0	$6,000	-99	$6,501
2	$6,501	$6,000	-206	$13,545
3	$13,545	$6,000	-322	$21,177
4	$21,177	$6,000	-448	$29,446
5	$29,446	$6,000	-585	$38,406
6	$38,406	$6,000	-733	$48,114
7	$48,114	$6,000	-893	$58,632
8	$58,632	$6,000	-1,066	$70,029
9	$70,029	$6,000	-1,254	$82,377
10	$82,377	$6,000	-1,458	$95,757
11	$95,757	$6,000	-1,679	$110,254
12	$110,254	$6,000	-1.918	$125,961
13	$125,961	$6,000	-2,177	$142,980
14	$142,980	$6,000	-2,458	$161,419
15	$161,419	$6,000	-2,762	$181,399

16	$181,399	$6,000	-3,092	$203,047
17	$203,047	$6,000	-3,449	$226,502
18	$226,502	$6,000	-3,836	$251,916
19	$251,916	$6,000	-4,256	$279,452
20	$279,452	$6,000	-4,710	$309,287
21	$309,287	$6,000	-5,202	$341,614
22	$341,614	$6,000	-5,736	$376,639
23	$376,639	$6,000	-6,314	$414,590
24	$414,590	$6,000	-6,940	$455,709
25	$455,709	$6,000	-7,618	$500,262
26	$500,262	$6,000	-8,353	$548,535
27	$548,535	$6,000	-9,150	$600,838
28	$600,838	$6,000	-10,013	$657,509
29	$657,509	$6,000	-10,948	$718,912
30	$718,912	$6,000	-11,961	$785,443
31	$785,443	$6,000	-13,059	$857,528
32	$857,528	$6,000	-14,537	$935,633
33	$935,633	$6,000	-15,537	$1,020,259
34	$1,020,259	$6,000	-16,933	$1,111,952
35	$1,111,952	$6,000	-18,446	**$1,211,300**
		Total	-197,862	-577,461

Jack could hardly believe his eyes. He'd gone into the exercise thinking of fees and commissions sort of like sales tax - no big deal. But now, he was on full alert. His once $1.8 million retirement had gone - fallen like the January thermometer - to just $1.2 million. Could it really be possible that fees and commissions would cost him a full *one-third* of what his account would grow to without those fees?

It was. Jack was moving from shocked - to angry. If his investment advisor had told him that his fees would cost him nearly $600,000 - well - it certainly would have changed the conversation when he'd hired him in the first place. And heck - those fees don't stop when Jack retires - they'll continue for the rest of his life - perhaps 55-60 years in all.

He met with his investment advisor and threw the spreadsheet on his desk, "$600,000, are you serious?" How many other clients was this guy hitting with over a half-million in fees? No wonder they all live like millionaires - they are! The advisor studied the table. "Look right here," he said reassuringly, "it's not $600,000 - its only $197,862." He relaxed - but Jack didn't.

He remembered his own analysis of the true impact of losses - and how everyone wanted him to focus on the growing account balance - *not* the fact that his seemingly insignificant 5% loss had really cost him 12.6% at the finish line. This kind of *"look over there - not over here"* sleight of hand had the same smell to it.

His advisor could take refuge behind the still huge - but comparatively tame figure of $200,000 if he wanted to - but Jack was catching on. Had the advisor not charged that $200,000 - Jack would have had all that $200k in his account - growing and compounding - and it would have netted him an extra - nearly $600,000 at the finish line.

He stormed out. What was he to do? He was beginning to question everything he'd been told and taught. His stomach was in knots. Then it dawned on him - he hadn't even gotten to the tax impact yet - and that one wasn't 1.5% - it was much worse.

Before moving on, Jack wanted to test one more nagging thought that had been rolling around in his brain since his whole "fee" analysis started. He wondered how much it would cost him to have deposited - and have his advisor manage that first $500 he ever put into his account - 35 years later.

So he took a single, solitary $500 deposit - and plugged it into his formula - growing it at 10% per annum, and charging 1.5% in fees and commissions against it each year. "Shock and awe" didn't begin to describe his reaction.

- 1.5% taken out of his $500 deposit, growing at 10%, over 35 years would cost **$1,537**.

- But that was just the gross figure. On to their game, he had to know what that $1,537 would have grown to if he had somehow been able to avoid it in the first place. Get this - leaving it to grow inside the account, that $1,537 would have turned into **$5,772**. That's right - the "opportunity cost" that he paid on a single $500 deposit was more than 10 times the amount of the deposit itself.

Lights blazing - and alarm bells ringing - and even though depression was setting in - he plowed forward. There was still one "beast" yet to quantify - taxes.

The Impact of Taxes

Feeling defeated and a bit nauseated, Jack chose not to speculate on what tax rates might be when he retires - that might push him right over the brink. So he made a decision to see what would happen to his $1.8 million account if he could avoid fees and commissions - and just had to face the "tax-music."

He decided to use a rather conservative rate of 25% on his gains, taxed annually. He knew the news would be bad - and braced himself for the result.

Year	Beginning Balance	New Savings	25% Tax On Gains	Ending Bal After Fees
1		$6,000	-150	$6,450
2	$6,450	$6,000	-311	$13,384
3	$13,384	$6,000	-485	$20,838
4	$20,838	$6,000	-671	$28,850
5	$28,850	$6,000	-871	$37,464
6	$37,464	$6,000	-1,087	$46,724
7	$46,724	$6,000	-1,318	$56,678
8	$56,678	$6,000	-1,567	$67,379
9	$78,883	$6,000	-1,834	$78,883
10	$78,883	$6,000	-2,122	$91,249
11	$91,249	$6,000	-2,431	$104,542
12	$104,542	$6,000	-2,764	$118,833
13	$118,833	$6,000	-3,121	$134,196
14	$134,196	$6,000	-3,505	$150,710
15	$150,710	$6,000	-3,918	$168,463
16	$168,463	$6,000	-4,362	$187,548
17	$187,548	$6,000	-4,839	$208,064
18	$208,064	$6,000	-5,352	$230,119
19	$230,119	$6,000	-5,903	$253,828
20	$253,828	$6,000	-6,496	$279,315
21	$279,315	$6,000	-7,133	$306,714

22	$306,714	$6,000	-7,818	$336,167
23	$336,167	$6,000	-8,554	$367,830
24	$367,830	$6,000	--9,346	$401,867
25	$401,867	$6,000	10,197	$438,457
26	$438,457	$6,000	-11,111	$477,791
27	$477,791	$6,000	-12,095	$520,076
28	$520,076	$6,000	-13,152	$565,532
29	$614,396	$6,000	-14,288	$614,396
30	$614,396	$6,000	-15,510	$666,926
31	$666,926	$6,000	-16,823	$723,396
32	$723,396	$6,000	-18,235	$784,100
33	$784,100	$6,000	-19,753	$849,358
34	$849,358	$6,000	-21,384	$919,510
35	$919,510	$6,000	-23,138	**$994,923**
		Total	**-261,641**	**-793,838**

Jack was less shocked than he'd expected. The total cost of taxes in gross dollars was **$261,461**, and the time value of those taxes - had they been avoidable and the money continued to grow in the account, was **$793,838**.

Perhaps he was a bit numb at this stage, but what surprised him was that the tax impact wasn't that much bigger than the drag of fees and commissions, which were $197,862 and **$577,461** respectively. To be sure, either number was enormous - but taxes at 25% had only a slightly greater impact than fees and commissions at 1.5%?

It was true. And what explained the difference was that the fees and commissions were assessed on the *entire* account - while taxes only applied to the *growth* on the account.

Jack's wife decided she'd chime in on the conversation. She had two points of dispute with Jack's analysis. First, she pointed out that a taxable account wouldn't necessarily pay taxes on the growth each year. It would only pay taxes when a position was sold at a gain. And investments held more than a year would qualify for capital gains treatment - a lower tax rate.

Jack explained that while she was technically right - he'd considered that in using a tax rate of just 25% - somewhere between the income tax rate - and the capital gains rate. He also reminded her that the majority of most people's accounts are held in mutual funds, which are *always* taxed as ordinary income - *never* as capital gains - even when held for more than one year.

She nodded in understanding - and told him how glad she was that she had chosen to build her wealth in the company 401(k) plan. Playing his best "Debbie Downer," Jack explained that the 401(k) plan didn't immunize her from the same outcome. Yes - there would arguably be more dollars going in, since she could contribute pre-tax dollars. And it was true that more dollars on the front end - would mean more dollars on the back-end - all things being equal. But Jack reminded her that none of those dollars had been taxed, so when they came out - it would be like the fees and commissions deduction - the entire balance would be taxed - and at a future rate they couldn't know.

As they both sat in silence - staring blankly at the floor - she wondered if that 401(k) plan had been such a good idea in the first place.

Putting it All Together
Depressed and angry, Jack's curiosity had the best of him. He just had to know what the cumulative effect of putting all three wealth eroders into the same analysis would look like. So he built one more spreadsheet - this time incorporating all three of the previously independent analysis.

- He interrupted the 35 year string of 10% gains, with three exceptions - flat (+/- 0) in years 14 and 32; and a 5% loss in year 22;

- He took out fees and commissions at the rate of 1.5% per year on the pre-tax balance; and

- He accounted for a 25% tax rate on gains after fees and commissions.

Yr	Begin Balance	New Savings	Growth Rate	1.5% Fees & Comm.'s	25%Tax on Gains	End Bal after Fees
1		$6,000	10%	($99)	($125)	$6,376
2	$6,376	$6,000	10%	($204)	($258)	$13,151
3	$13,151	$6,000	10%	($316)	($400)	$20,350
4	$20,350	$6,000	10%	($435)	($550)	$28,000
5	$28,000	$6,000	10%	($561)	($710)	$36,130

6	$36,130	$6,000	10%	($695)	($879)	$44,768
7	$44,768	$6,000	10%	($838)	($1,060)	$53,947
8	$53,947	$6,000	10%	($989)	($1,251)	$63,701
9	$63,701	$6,000	10%	($1,150)	($1,455)	$74,066
10	$74,066	$6,000	10%	($1,321)	($1,671)	$85,081
11	$85,081	$6,000	10%	($1,503)	($1,901)	$96,785
12	$96,785	$6,000	10%	($1,696)	($2,146)	$109,221
13	$109,221	$6,000	10%	($1,901)	($2,405)	$122,437
14	$122,437	46,000	0%	($1,927)	$0	$126,511
15	$126,511	$6,000	10%	($2,186)	($2,766)	$140,809
16	$140,809	$6,000	10%	($2,422)	($3,065)	$156,003
17	$156,003	$6,000	10%	($2,673)	($3,382)	$172,148
18	$172,148	$6,000	10%	($2,939)	($3,719)	$189,305
19	$189,305	$6,000	10%	($3,223)	($4,077)	$207,536
20	$207,536	$6,000	10%	($3,523)	($4,458)	$226,909
21	$226,909	$6,000	10%	($3,843)	($4,862)	$247,495
22	$247,495	$6,000	-5%	($3,612)	$0	$237,208
23	$237,208	$6,000	10%	($4,013)	($5,077)	$258,438
24	$258,438	$6,000	10%	($4,363)	($5,520)	$280,999
25	$280,999	$6,000	10%	($4,735)	($5,991)	$304,972
26	$304,972	$6,000	10%	($5,131)	($6,492)	$330,447
27	$330,447	$6,000	10%	($5,551)	($7,023)	$357,517
28	$357,517	$6,000	10%	($5,998)	($7,588)	$386,282
29	$386,282	$6,000	10%	($6,473)	($8,189)	$416,849
30	$416,849	$6,000	10%	($6,977)	($8,827)	$449,330
31	$449,330	$6,000	10%	($7,513)	($9,505)	$483,845
32	$483,845	$6,000	0%	($7,348)	$0	$482,497
33	$482,497	$6,000	10%	($8,060)	($10,197)	$519,089
34	$519,089	$6,000	10%	($8,664)	($10,961)	$557,973
35	$557,973	$6,000	10%	($9,306)	($11,773)	$599,292
				($122,189)	($138,284)	($1,189,469)

There it was - staring him in the face. He wouldn't be retiring on $1.8 million, but rather just one-third of that amount - $599,292. That meant that all the work - all the sacrifice - all the efforts he expended to earn a very respectable 10% on his money (in all but three years) would come down to $600,000?

And all that based on a set of rather conservative assumptions:

- Just three years in 35 that broke the 10% annual growth rate
- A fee and commission deduction of just 1.5%, and
- A blended tax rate of just 25% on the growth only.

He sat in disbelief. Was this really how it worked? Was this why almost everyone in the financial services community had nice offices, fancy houses, and lived the good life? Did the whole mainstream wealth-building proposition come down to this?

> *You put up all the money - You take all the risk - and for that - you get a third of the total amount of money that's generated from your 35 years of effort.*

Hard as it was to believe - it was true. No wonder everybody talks only about offense - what they can do to grow our money. They have to if they're going to have a chance of overcoming the ball and chain of the three wealth-eroders. Besides, if they let us truly understand the impact of the wealth-eroders the way Jack had analyzed them - nobody would put their money in traditional markets - through traditional advisors and brokers.

When it was all said and done - Jack wondered why no one had ever shared any of this valuable information with him before - not his parents, his professors, his friends, his associates, not the trade publications he read or the media gurus he watched and listened to - not Dave Ramsey, Suze Orman, Jim Kramer - or the others.

Maybe the mainstream-investing world wasn't the best route for him. Maybe it wasn't the best for anyone. Jack gained new energy as he resolved to find a better way. A way where there **is no risk of market loss** - but where he wouldn't have to give up growth potential either. A way that **didn't suffer the impact of fees and commissions.** And a way **that was tax-free.**

Could there be such a thing? There is - and it's been hiding in plain sight for decades. The "World's Way" will not be Jack's way anymore. How about you?

Rigged

Appendix 2

Case Studies

Throughout this book, I've provided you with a great deal of information from which you can begin to draw your own conclusions. I've also shown you a different way of building wealth. A way that avoids the Three Failure Traps. A way that perfectly attends our two rules of investing: *Failure is not an Option*, and *First, Lose No Money*. And a way that meets all the Five Money Needs of Safety, Growth, Income, Liquidity, and Tax-Efficiency.

My solution is the use of equity-indexed universal life insurance. Perhaps you may be leaning my way - but you're not quite there yet. The theory sounds good - but how would this really apply to you?

Those answers can only come from a seasoned life insurance professional - not the one in the phone book, and not the one that can take care of your car and your house - but one focused on life insurance and annuity products exclusively. So to give you a glimpse of what that might end up looking like, let's look at two case studies.

Huey, Louie, and Dewey

Huey, Louie, and Dewey are all 30 years old. They have good jobs, and are committed to saving $500/month from now, until they retire at age 65. All three are going to earn 8% on their money the entire time.

Huey uses a taxable account because he wants access to his money if he needs it. So while he starts out with $500/month, he only has $400/month to invest after taxes.

Louie is smart. He takes advantage of his company 401(k) plan and puts the full $500/month in. His company is generous, and matches Louie's contributions at a rate of 50% - meaning every time Louie puts in $500, the company adds $250.

Dewey read the book, and decides to put his money into equity-indexed universal life insurance. Like Huey, he has to make after-tax contributions, so he only gets the benefit of $400 going into his plan.

Huey, Louie, and Dewey all meet up on their 65th birthday to celebrate life, and compare notes. Here's what they learn:

	Huey	Louie	Dewey
After-Tax Cash at Retirement	$520,302	$849,708	$1,028,673
After-Tax Income to age 100	$37,556	$61,333	$139,789
Total Income Drawn by Age 85	$751,121	$1,226,660	$2,795,780
"Legacy" Balance at age 85	$237,901	$597,719	$506,053
Total Lifetime Value of Plan	$989,022	$1,824,379	$3,301,833

Now if that doesn't get you off the couch and in search of a good life insurance professional, I don't know what will.

Jack and Jill

Jack and Jill are both 50. They've both built up nice qualified plan account balances that are identical. They're both still saving money, but now - in their peak earning years - they're saving at a rate of $1,000/month. They both read this book. Jack dismissed much of the information. It wasn't so much that he didn't believe it - he did. But Jack figured that at age 50, life insurance would be much more expensive than it would have been at 35 - so in his mind - the window of opportunity for him to leverage the power of cash-value life insurance was in the rearview mirror. Besides, the company matched 100% of Jack's contributions, up to $500/month. So instead, he continued to plow down the qualified plan path.

After meeting with her insurance agent, Jill learned that the advantages of properly structured life insurance plans *do not diminish with age*. Sure, the cost of the insurance component would be higher per $1,000 of life insurance benefit she bought - but at age 50, she didn't have to buy nearly as much life insurance as she would have at age 35. So the bottom line is that she can do just as well with a life insurance plan at 50 - as she could at 35.

Despite the fact that she would be giving up those employer matching funds, Jill decided to stop putting money into the qualified plan altogether, and put the full $1,000/month into a well structured indexed universal life insurance plan.

Let's freeze their accumulated qualified plan balances since they're identical; and focus instead only on what happens to the money they save from today - age 50, to their retirement at age 65.

194

	Jack	Jill
After-Tax Cash at Retirement	$292,753	$276,305
After-Tax Income that will last to age 100	$19,668	$35,408
Total After-Tax Income Drawn by Age 85	$393,366	$708,160
"Legacy" Balance in Account at age 85	$199,136	$126,039
Total Lifetime Value of Plan (Income to 85 + Legacy)	$592,502	$834,199

Jill's total plan value - which is the sum of the income she would draw through age 85, and the remaining account balance she would pass on at age 85, is more than 40% greater than Jacks. So the assumption that life insurance is only for the young, is totally wrong.

Clearly, both case studies have to make certain assumptions about the cost of fees and commissions, and tax rates at retirement. Both used very reasonable assumptions - a cost of fees and commissions of 1.5% per year, and a combined federal, state, and local tax rate at retirement of 35%.

I hope a stark, and hopeful message has emerged for you. I hope the mysterious veil of life insurance and the strong reaction it has a tendency to elicit, have given way to fact and rationality.

If markets always cooperated with our growth objectives and our investing timeline; if governments didn't feel a need to constantly tinker with how much of our money should actually be ours; if our advisers would impose reasonable fees that were clear up front; perhaps all I've laid out for you would be unnecessary. But it is not. And the conclusion I've arrived at is that Equity-Indexed Life Insurance is the most powerful, and certain wealth-building pathway there is.

If you're moving toward the same conclusion, I urge you to seek out a life insurance professional and have a conversation about how all this could be put to work for you.

Rigged

Appendix 3

Ten Questions

Let me leave you with this. Much of what we've shared in these pages may seem so counter-intuitive that it borders on the unbelievable. If all this is true, why are you just now hearing about it? Why don't all the famous sources of financial knowledge talk about this kind of thing? Is this guy right - and the whole financial services industry wrong?

These are questions you'll have to answer on your own as you seek to validate - or invalidate, what I've shared with you. But in doing so, I challenge you to reflect on the following 10 questions. Do so with an open mind, and serious discernment. I believe they'll help you move your mind one way or the other.

1. How much of your money did you give your advisor permission to lose?
2. Does your advisor know how much income you want in retirement, when it should start, and how long you want it to last?
3. How certain are you that all planning steps have been taken to avoid having your social security benefits taxed?
4. How certain are you that all planning steps have been taken to avoid losing assets to Medicaid spend-down?
5. How certain are you that you'll have enough money available for assisted living and/or nursing home expenses?
6. How certain are you that you've taken the proper planning steps so that your estate avoids probate?
7. Will your IRA, 401(k), or other qualified accounts pass to your intended heirs with its tax-deferred status intact?
8. Will your estate be subject to estate and inheritance taxes?
9. Is it important for you to know – with certainty – the answers to the first 8 questions?
10. What are you going to do about getting the answers – who, when, how?